Your SOUL METAMORPHOSIS

DARK NIGHT OF THE SOUL

YOUR UNEXPLAINED SUFFERING HAPPENS WHEN GOD'S HAND IS AT WORK

TRINITY ROYAL

DARK NIGHT OF THE SOUL

YOUR SOUL METAMORPHOSIS. YOUR UNEXPLAINED SUFFERING HAPPENS WHEN GOD'S HAND IS AT WORK

TRINITY ROYAL

CONTENTS

Library of Congress Control Number: 2022901725

SPECIAL BONUS – FREE BOOKS TO OUR READERS

Free books to our readers

War in Heaven came to Earth. Satan Rebellion:

https://dl.bookfunnel.com/ea12ys3dmk

Your Life in Heaven:

https://dl.bookfunnel.com/vg451qpuzs

INTRODUCTION

"There can be no rebirth without a Dark Night of the Soul, a total annihilation of all that you believed in and thought that you were."— Hazrat Inayat Khan.

The physical body that you currently inhabit also embodies your soul. The soul is the deepest and most complete expression of a person. Your real and true identity is your soul. Every soul that has ever existed in its creation is unique and identifiable by its soul signature, which is as distinctive as a fingerprint.

The purpose of your soul's existence is to have experiences and to grow into its fullest expression. As you grow through different stages of life, you are influenced by your surroundings, including the people and places you come into contact with.

Power is constantly flowing throughout the universe, and the soul is bathed in this constant flow of energy. What you choose to do with the energy determines your soul's experiences. Some of your experiences contribute to your soul's growth and development, while other experiences might not. The soul experiences a multitude of trials and tribulations along its journey. You might wonder where your soul is journeying, and the answer is that your soul is on a quest to enrich itself and then return back to its source of origin in the universe. The universe is structured to assist your soul in making choices. In a way, the universe is in a conspiracy for your soul's growth, as it is in the world's favor for you to grow fully into your soul's potential.

During this journey, your soul has acquired—and will continue to acquire—various experiences, both good and bad, favorable and unfavorable, positive and negative. However, to continue its journey back to the source of its creation, all of the residual bad, unfavorable, negative energy has to be discarded. When you shed that negative residue, your energetic vibration will be high enough for your soul to endure the frequencies of the higher realms. This shedding of negative energies usually involves some type of suffering. This comes to each and every Soul at some point in the soul journey.

The bad news is: We are the creators of our suffering.

The good news is: We are the creators of our suffering.

Most of the suffering that we see is self-made or environment or bad decisions and or Karmic in nature. There are some solutions for these categories of suffering. However, there is a type of suffering that I call "righteous suffering." This is also called "The Dark Night of the Soul." The roots of this type of suffering are Spiritual in nature. This righteous suffering has a definite and clear purpose. The purpose is Soul growth.

The Dark Night of the Soul is a spiritual desolation, the length of which depends on who the Soul is, its journey, the Soul's choices, and the necessity of Soul service on Earth at this time. It is very important to understand this.

Although it is difficult to determine the nature of the cause of Dark Night of the Soul, here are some main differences that delineate between regular suffering vs. Dark Night of the Soul.

What exactly happens during Dark Night of the Soul:

- This is a spiritual isolation of the Soul

- The person usually experiences great stress, loss, pain, anxiety, loss of self, and loss of everything one holds dear How long will this last?

- DNOS can last for many months to many years to decades. The duration depends on the Soul. The soul choices, experiences, nature of the journey, environment, who the Soul is and its purpose, and also the service requirements on Earth at this time. So, the answer is, "It depends." This is up to Divine discretion.

What happens at the end of Dark Night of the Soul?

- You are completely transformed. You have graduated to the next phase of your evolution. You have shed those parts of you that no longer serve you. Your Soul has become lighter and is vibrating at higher frequencies. You have become closer to Spirit/God.

The Dark Night of the Soul is an essential rite of passage. But when it arrives, it is soul-sucking. Everything is meaningless because all of a sudden, the previous meaning we gave our lives proves insufficient. Perhaps you've achieved the wealth you wanted, only to discover it doesn't buy happiness. Perhaps you put all of your value into a relationship that crumpled in the end. Maybe you achieved your dreams just to discover that it doesn't seem right in the end. This is a dreadful realization, but it also marks the beginning of a life altering metamorphosis. If you're strong enough to lean into the experience, with strength and curiosity, you'll come out the other side healed and with new, renewed strength.

If you're reading this, you may have already experienced a crossroads like the one I'm describing. Some people have many dark nights of the soul because the soul is always evolving. That's precisely what our souls are meant to do—evolve. So, if you've recently experienced a great amount of loss, or an odd surge of depression, understand that this is the beginning as much as it is an ending. And you now have the power to embrace life on a deeper level. You've been called to grow and transform. And once you face your fears, you'll discover a deeper connection to your truth, your heart, and the magic of the universe in which we are intrinsically linked. You'll discover your soul once more, and what's more worthwhile than that?

Divine Hands will guide you and transform you. This is a great blessing to you and your loved ones.

When your Dark Night of the Soul ends (and it will end eventually), your former life is unrecognizable. Little remains the same. Not only do you feel better and recategorize your life as an incredible experience, but you think better, relate better, and connect with God better.

This book will dive deeper into the Dark Night of the Soul process and how it unfolds externally and internally, what happens when you are going through the process, and your Metamorphosis during this time. We will also focus on the things that can help you during the arduous process, to-dos, and not-to-dos, including many healing techniques that can be of great help during your journey. This will help facilitate your soul's journey into the higher frequencies on your way back home to the source.

There is a story behind every person who made a significant positive contribution to society. We see only the visible part of them; there are tears, sweat, and blood that most rarely realize. This is their Metamorphosis through the DNOS journey. Are you on the list?

The info and techniques presented in this book are general and can help anyone who needs answers to the nature of suffering and how to heal themselves.

DNOS journey is your blessing in disguise.

WHY YOUR SOUL JOURNEY MATTERS

"Our Soul knows the geography of your destiny. Your soul alone has the map of your future; therefore, you can trust this indirect, oblique side of yourself. If you do, it will take you where you need to." – John O'Donohue.

I n today's modern society, there is much emphasis on personality typology, mental health, and seeking answers through psychology. These systems are all helpful and wonderful, but they often fail to address the larger piece within our life's epic puzzle, the piece that reveals a deeper, more spiritual connection to the profundity of life. It's that thing that motivates us after tragedies and appears like dreams in our high-spirited youths. It's the soul, forever enduring and wise. The soul is your compass, your purpose, and your tether to the world's undercurrents. It's that thing that nudges you on a path toward fulfillment, even when family, friends, or society try to push you elsewhere. It's that part of you that has survived millennia, not through your current physical form, but through spirit. And if you listen to its subtle yet demanding messages, you will discover a survival mechanism, a support that has the power to guide you through any and all darkness. You will also discover an original path, one that leads to the promise of fulfillment. That is why the soul's journey is so significant.

The soul's journey is one that can't be tracked by a calendar.

It consists of many lifetimes, stretching over centuries of lived life. It embodies not only your physical existence, with all your conscious decisions and choices, but also your spiritual existence—the deeper meanings behind those choices. Every person's soul is unique, just as every human being is unique. Therefore, no two paths look the same. But each one of us has a soul, nonetheless, and a journey through which to develop it. For example, each of us is born with certain strengths and weaknesses, certain innate talents and challenges. These are the qualities that reveal our soul's path. It's not a matter of pondering one's purpose, then sticking with that come hell or high water. It's about living an experience that embraces your unique skill set. It's about staying true to yourself—your core self — and building a life based on your deepest desires. It isn't about taking advice from a psychic or oracle; rather, it's the intuitive encouragement that manifests through our own free will. Whatever we decide to do, so long as it's born out of genuine desire, reveals our soul's purpose. We have the power to create it just by living through our passions and interests. It's not chosen for us. We color it ourselves.

This is why self-reflection is so important. To live by your soul's purpose, you don't need to take a "True Vocations Quiz." You simply need to turn inward, have important conversations with yourself, and learn everything there is to know about your true identity. Once that internal work is done, you'll never have to worry about whether you're on the right path. The path unfolds naturally, along with self-understanding. All we have to do is muster the courage and confidence to live by our own rules, our internal compass. And it isn't selfish to do this! Self-understanding is the key to a happy and fulfilling life. So, take the time to focus on yourself, your needs, and your dreams. That's the only way to make contact with the soul.

Once you do make contact with your soul, you may experience certain roadblocks on the path toward spiritual fulfillment. These usually come in the form of psychological hangups like childhood trauma, struggles with self-esteem, relationship issues, and emotional instability. Every journey includes some obstacles, and the soul's journey is no different. These are the issues that give the soul strength. Through overcoming our psychological limitations, we deepen our relationships with ourselves and gain enough strength and wisdom to persevere on our chosen paths. If self-knowledge is the key to happiness and fulfillment, then the inevitable setbacks may be nothing more than necessary nudges, like a trail of breadcrumbs that leads to a deeper understanding and purpose.

Think about it this way... life cannot be reduced to a single, physical incarnation. It's a massive web that we cannot begin to understand completely, no matter how desperately we try. So, our soul's growth does not depend on achieving our dream jobs, marrying our soul mates, or completing the highest level of education. If these societal constructs provided the impetus to our soul's journey, everyone would be much more content in life. But the soul is less concerned with achievement and more concerned with curiosity. It wants to learn. Through learning, true growth occurs, and through growth, we ascend to higher spiritual octaves. We set ourselves up properly for our next lifetime, and we contribute to the overall growth of the human collective. In this way, life is really a school, a metaphorical educational system for our souls to learn everything there is to know about how to truly LIVE. Our souls are continuously enrolled in the School of Life. And it is through engaging in the learning process that we can nurture our souls to their fullest capacities.

Additionally, whatever lessons our souls cannot fully grasp within this lifetime can be further explored during the next lifetime. We aren't taught this in school when we learn about the planets and the Big Bang, but our lives and all of creation are infinite. According to expert Sam Boomer, "It's easy to limit our perception of what's possible to what's in front of us. But the totality of creation extends far beyond our Earth, our Solar System, and even beyond the universal level we exist on. Creation is an infinite concept that knows no bounds."

No one individual can understand the vastness of life, no matter how hard they try. So, it's not surprising that so many people grapple with the concept of infiniteness. We live on a relatively small planet, following the rules of our small society and putting much focus on our day-to-day tasks and responsibilities. This doesn't leave much room for existential musings. But the galaxy in which we live is more expansive than we can ever comprehend, and our souls are an intrinsic part of that expansiveness.

Just like humans evolved from apes and apes evolved from fish, we, too, are in a perpetual state of evolution. Our souls evolve with every life that passes. We choose, with each life, the challenges and circumstances our soul requires to develop and mature more fully. Most soul experts believe that we choose this of our own free will. And the more we listen to the intuitive messages from our souls, the faster we evolve. Our souls can take us in a variety of directions—through life as different races, living on different planets in vastly different vocations and lifestyles. It's all in the name of progress, both on an individual level and a collective level, as the larger organism of which we are all apart. That takes us to the idea of infinite existence. If life has been evolving for centuries, it's safe to say that we have already mastered certain things... survival, for one. We've learned how to stay alive, how to connect from opposite sides of the planet, and how to share knowledge and communicate. So, what is the collective goal now? What do our souls require at this stage of development?

Now, through the infiniteness of existence, we are learning how to love unconditionally. In other words, whenever you practice self-love or perform acts of selfless love for others, you're raising your soul's vibration. You're working to achieve the highest level of soul growth possible during this incarnation. That may sound like a lot of pressure, but it's actually impossible to mess it up. No matter what you decide to do in life, your soul will learn lessons. As humans, we can't help but learn from everything we do. And so long as we're learning, we're making progress. So, lean into the experience of infiniteness. Let your soul try things and learn from those things over and over again. And remember to love not only those around you but also yourself. It is said that our souls are currently tackling the 3rd dimension, which is all about love. So, all we have to do in this lifetime is follow our hearts the way we would a trusted parent or guide.

In order to "believe" in a soul's journey, you do not have to reject free will. Free will is an intrinsic part of the soul's journey. All of life is a series of choices. We make those choices using our own freedom of thought and action. There's no one telling us to do one thing over the other. There is no god controlling your actions like you're an avatar in a computer game. We make choices based on our natural dispositions and uniqueness. Then, those choices form the groundwork for your soul's journey. We can apply this to our physical incarnations, of course. You choose to take one job. You choose to get married or stay single. You choose to live in one city over another. These are all soul choices that we make consciously as living, breathing human beings. But there are other choices we make between incarnations, choices that are also a product of our own free will. These choices require more existential coordination because they're the choices that decide the psychological framework of our next life.

Many believe that we have ample time between lives to coordinate the various things we need for further soul progress. For example, if you devoted your last life to career success, you might wish to level your karma and devote your next life to more private matters. You then assess what obstacles and drama your soul will require to develop this area of life. You have the opportunity to collude with your "soul group" so that the other important people in your life can act as important characters in your journey. Your mother in this lifetime might be your best friend in the next. She might help you in different ways, depending on your lifetime and the current needs of your soul. But this is all decided in the unconscious space between physical incarnations. It's still a form of free will; it's just simply inaccessible in our physical, bodily forms.

Your soul's journey is important because growth is the meaning of life. Life cannot exist without growth, and growth cannot exist without life. Without the soul's journey, there would be no progress. There would be no human bodies. There would be no passion, love, or sense of togetherness. It gives new meaning to the phrase, "Everything happens for a reason." Our lives and the circumstances we are born to exist for a specific reason—we chose them on a soul level. There are certain lessons we need to learn based on our circumstances, and somewhere deep down, we all know this. And if we are wise, we make the most out of our scenarios with tenacity and curiosity.

Your Soul Calling, Purpose, and Destiny

"There is no greater gift you can give or receive than to honor your (soul) calling. It's why you were born. And how you become most truly alive." – Oprah Winfrey

We've already established that our soul's journey reflects a profound choice, a choice that each of us makes before we enter the consciousness of our physical bodies. This begs an obvious question—why do we choose a specific journey? What motivates us to choose one life theme over the other, and how does that affect the larger organism of which we are a part? We're all connected through energy, and every human being has the unique opportunity to affect other human beings that they come into contact with. Our purpose serves a larger purpose.

So why, then, do some of us choose a path that leads to great leadership while others choose to make waves through more private methods? Why do some people choose challenges and heartache when they could easily choose an easier journey? No life is without its challenges, but why do some souls choose to step directly into the fire? If every soul's journey is about growth, perhaps those souls who choose particularly difficult paths are the same souls who are the most dedicated to growing. It takes courage to grow. And if we look at each soul's journey through that lens of courageousness, we can alter our view of heartache and darkness. And we can shed light on the profundity and massive impact of the soul's journey.

It's impossible to understand the deeper meaning of the soul's journey without first exploring the issue of karma. Karma is essentially the idea of cause and effect. If you perform an action that is "good," you should receive a good result. By contrast, if you perform an action that is "bad," you will receive a bad result. Karma is popular in many religions and often forms the foundation for moral doctrines and philosophies. The idea that what we give is what we receive can be applied to a wide variety of systems and functions. If you water a plant, for example, you can expect it to grow. If you compliment a new friend, there's a good chance they'll return the sentiment. If you antagonize someone, they'll likely return with harsh words of their own. There's an energetic transaction that occurs constantly all around us. If you look closely, you'll notice how karma plays a role in nature, in relationships, in fictional stories, and, of course, in reincarnation.

It's impossible to grow without embracing cause and effect. Any time we perform an action, we are also fated to encounter the effects of that action. However, some people choose to live through awareness of karma, while others choose to dismiss it.

Growth is more fulfilling and productive when we perform our actions with an awareness of karma. When we live through the knowledge that good intentions breed good results, we set ourselves up for a life of abundance. Challenges are still inevitable, but we can manage them better because we know that with integrity and positivity, the chips will fall in our favor once more.

Sometimes, our karmic results are immediate, and other times, they take a lifetime to come back to us. The process of reincarnation has close links with karma because whatever we decide to do in our current life has the propensity to affect our next life, and so on and so forth. "According to Tenzin Lama, in 'true' karma, positive actions receive happiness, and negative actions receive suffering. Negative action comes from speech, body, and mind. Saying something unkind, physically fighting or killing, and feeling jealousy are all examples of negative action." So, these actions may affect the circumstances of our future lives for better or worse. The good news is that we always have the ability to redirect our karma if we have accumulated too much negativity. There's always the opportunity to change our fortunes through the intention of goodwill.

Now, it's easy to assume that karma is like a force from God. If you believe in a punishing higher power, you may have a skewed interpretation of karma. Karma isn't the universal punishment for bad behavior. It's more nuanced than that… or perhaps it's more simplistic. You can think of karma much like gravity. It's a principle more than a mystical force. In terms of the soul's journey, however, karma comes in the form of lessons. Remember that we choose our life themes before we physically incarnate into our bodies. We choose those life themes based on the karmic lessons we must learn. Therefore, karma is not a punishment from a higher power but a rite of passage that we hand-select. We choose what we need to endure in order to achieve balance and growth. Problems arise when we have the wrong mindset about these karmic challenges.

If we only view our karmic lessons from a victim mentality, then we can't allow our souls the growth they need. It's impossible. In order to achieve growth, we have to lean into our life's challenges. We must face them head-on rather than reject them or wish our lives were different. Our karmic power arrives when we fight against our challenges in the name of growth. Remember, you can only wait in the dark for so long. Enduring is the only way through, and once you do get through, you'll experience light which offers newfound fulfillment and peace. This is where the Dark Night of the Soul comes in.

Spiritual counselor Mateo Sol said, "The Dark Night of the Soul is a period of utter spiritual desolation, disconnection, and emptiness in which one feels totally separated from the Divine." This experience arrives for everyone at some point in life. The truth is that in our modern society, we are not encouraged to live through our souls. Instead, we're propelled to live through our egos. We're encouraged to invest our lives in money, superficial versions of success, and relationships that don't even fulfill us. Some people have children just because they're seeking purpose and meaning that they otherwise cannot obtain... or so they think. Additionally, when hardship arrives, many of us are taught that we must bury our depression and get back to work. "Just keep yourself busy" is a popular phrase people echo. But what if our darkest days actually serve as the catalyst to our highest fulfillment? What if the hardship isn't something that should be glossed over with expensive items and a new romantic fling? What if the hardship reveals our power... and, furthermore, our destinies?

When hardship arrives, it's usually a sign that we need to grow in some way. We need to take accountability for our divine potential. We need to get up every morning and consider the different ways we can live through our souls rather than society or other people's expectations. The Dark Night of the Soul refers to more than just a rough day or a difficult week. The Dark Night of the Soul points to something more profound and spiritual. It occurs when we find ourselves exceptionally lost. It's like a spiritual emergency. A voice whispers to us from somewhere deep inside, asking, *'What is the point of all of this?'* and *'What am I living for?'* These are the intuitive yearnings that crystallize the dark night. And although it's dark and painful, it's also a spiritual nudge toward a brighter light.

So how does this nudge reveal our destinies? Once we can identify our experience as a Dark Night of the Soul. How do we walk toward the light rather than wallow in self-pity or supplant the sadness through petty ego attachments?

Well, if you're asking yourself those questions I mentioned earlier, then you're on your way to reuniting with your soul. And once you reunite with your soul, your deeper purpose is revealed. During this "dark night," which may actually be a dark year or a few dark months, you will ask yourself the hard questions. 'Why am I here?' and 'How can I live in a more deeply satisfying way?' Often, these questions are the culmination of several events. Perhaps your partner left you, you lost a job, a loved one passed, or all your friends are moving away. It may seem as if life pulled the rug out from under you. But there is always a deeper meaning to these events. It just means that it's time to heal through the roots of your being.

The Dark Night of the Soul is actually the thing that can progress your cycle of karmic evolution. If handled correctly, it's the point where your karma can change. Once you've reached the bottom of the bottom, you can only go up. This is different from depression, of course. Depression can linger as a product of childhood abuse or neglect. It can be a result of certain circumstances, and it can be cured through therapy or lifestyle changes. The Dark Night of the Soul is a more significant rite of passage that everyone must endure. It's a spiritual or existential issue, and it can't be cured through a change of lifestyle alone. It requires consciousness and a recommitment to spiritual wholeness. Depression doesn't always prompt an ego death, but the Dark Night of the Soul, if handled the right way, leaves you utterly transformed. Your ego dies to be reborn anew.

In order to be born anew, we have to let certain things go. Transformation requires a kind of death, and it usually starts with our egos because our egos don't serve our souls. Once we relinquish the ego, once we lose the things that are meant to be lost, and once we embrace the emptiness that is a by-product of the dark night, we can re-familiarize ourselves with what lies underneath. In that moment of depletion, we realize that the emptiness contains a message—peace lies in existence, not in external things. Even when our tanks are empty, we can access deeper happiness, a contentment that is always with us if we just allow ourselves to relax, breathe, and be. This is when we discover that happiness isn't this thing or that thing. It just *is*.

As Mateo Sol said, "Those that have experienced or are currently experiencing a Dark Night of the Soul will know that something very fundamental at a core level is out of focus or completely lacking in their lives. Those going through a Dark Night will sense that so much more is possible in their lives, even though they don't exactly know what that '*so much more*' is." (Sol, 2022).

So, you see, the Dark Night of the Soul is profoundly useful on a number of levels. It's an opportunity for deepened spiritual growth. And while it's objectively painful, the pain offers permanent gain. Like a caterpillar that transforms into a butterfly, the transformation process is dark and necessary, but the resulting wings allow the creature to fly high for the remainder of its life. The Dark Night of the Soul also teaches humility and grace. It often shows us that we can't control everything, and that process of letting go of control can be immensely relieving. And once you've released, you can enjoy the abundance that arrives. Your willpower will be strengthened because your natural path will reveal itself. Your faith in life will be restored, and your determination will be kicked into high gear.

That's the thing about destiny and determination—it often needs loss to find a voice. For example, I went through a breakup that left me feeling empty. I invested years into a person who, when all was said and done, decided to leave the country and pursue a solo life without me. This brought devastation and emptiness. It was as if a part of me had been sucked away, never to return. I was lonely, isolated, and lifeless. Nothing excited me anymore, and all my motivation was lost. But after enough time passed, I built a new relationship with myself and with my soul. I started living for myself and embracing the small things in life— the view while driving to work, a moving poem found on social media—and at a certain point, I found that glow again. By living in the present moment, I find excitement and inspiration once more. I had space to discover my purpose because I wasn't attached to other things. This is how the dark night reveals meaning. It can steer your life in a completely different direction based on whatever conscious choices you make from your new perspective. It's like cleaning out an old vase full of dying flowers. You have to remove the old flowers, clean out the vase, and find something new and beautiful to replace it with. But often, the inspiration doesn't arrive until you're looking at the clean and empty vase.

It's not like a voice appears on our darkest nights from high above. There is no instruction manual on how to find your purpose once all is lost. But if you live from your heart when all the chips are down. If you make conscious choices that reflect your soul's deepest yearnings, you'll find your purpose through whatever you are drawn to. You'll discover what makes your heart sing, and you'll find the strength to reorient your life based on that. It promises massive rewards of a deeply fulfilling nature. If you sit with your heart in the darkness, your destiny will emerge. So long as you pick yourself up and go after the things that *you* want. Don't listen to anyone else. Do the things that bring you joy, and joy will flood your system like a spiritual tsunami.

WHY DOES SUFFERING HAPPEN

"There is no coming to consciousness without pain. People will do anything, no matter how absurd, to avoid facing their own souls. One does not become enlightened by imagining figures of light, but by making the darkness conscious" – Carl Gustav Jung.

C uriosity is the single factor for the Soul to undergo most experiences. Some of these experiences add value to the Soul by raising its vibrations, whereas some not-so-good experiences reduce the vibrations of the soul.

It is in the Human DNA of every ensouled being to grow in spirit and become closer to the source of its truth. Hence the journey is a natural by-product of every ensouled Human being.

When the Soul is ready to take its journey back to the source, it has to go through a shedding process of removing energies that are not helping to raise its vibrations. This journey is what we have called Dark Night of the Soul. So why is it Dark Night? It is because, most of the time, this shedding of negative energies involves pain and suffering. Rarely growth happens without pain.

Clearing negative energies from your mind and enriching it with positive experiences that align with your Soul is your DNOS journey. This is your Metamorphosis.

Mind and Soul are connected. The soul is considered the essence of man, while the mind is in charge of man's consciousness and thoughts.

Let's dissect a bit deeper into why the pain/suffering or Dark Nights happen. This involves some understanding of how our mental and emotional selves are made.

Your brain is a vastly interesting object. It is likely one of the most complex things in the universe. The brain is the house of Mind., Scientists agree there are two distinct yet connected systems: the conscious mind and the subconscious mind.

The conscious mind is your logical mind. It receives information from your five senses. It is where you think and rationalize. Logic rules the day in the conscious mind. However, the conscious mind does not control our actions.

Our actions are almost exclusively controlled by the subconscious mind. This mind is largely ruled by emotions and instinct. Its job is to help us meet our needs and urges: reproduction, food, thirst, safety, intimacy, and many others. It is a very powerful force. It doesn't reason or judge; it simply acts, often commanding your actions.

Together, these two minds work together to determine your actions. They can bring you success or failure, happiness or anxiety, achievement or frustration. It is all in the way you use them.

The subconscious mind is a data bank for everything which is not in your conscious mind. It stores your beliefs, your previous experience, your memories, and your skills. Everything that you have seen, done, or thought about is also there. This storehouse contains all information that you have experienced since your inception or since your soul's birth. This could be a long time.

Communicating thoughts from your conscious mind to your subconscious mind is difficult because it should be done with emotions. Only the thoughts that are conveyed with genuine emotions make it to the back of your mind. And only the thoughts that are backed up by a strong emotion stay there.

Unfortunately, this is true both for the negative and the positive emotions. The negative emotions are usually stronger than the positive ones.

Self-Development Author Brian Or summarizes the importance of the subconscious mind:

'Let's first take a moment to consider the fact that your subconscious mind is like a huge memory bank. Its capacity is virtually unlimited, and it permanently stores everything that ever happens to you. By the time you reach the age of 21, you've already permanently stored more than one hundred times the contents of the entire Encyclopedia Britannica.

Under hypnosis, older people can often remember, with perfect clarity, events from fifty years before. Your unconscious memory is virtually perfect. It is your conscious recall that is suspect.

Clearing negative energies from your Conscious and Subconscious mind and enriching it with positive experiences that align with your Soul is your DNOS journey. This is your Metamorphosis.

Ice Berg Model

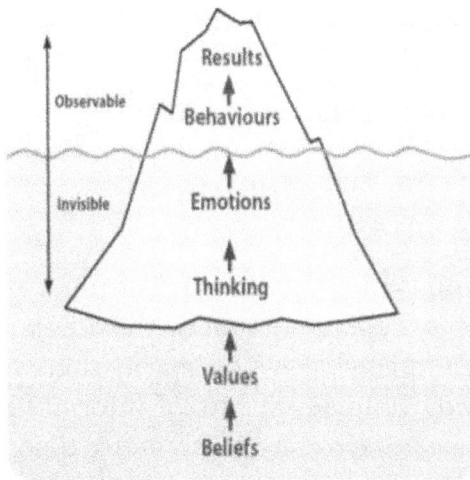

An iceberg can serve as a useful model to understand the unconscious mind, its relationship to the conscious mind, and how the two parts of our minds work together.

As an iceberg floats in the water, a huge mass of it remains below the surface. Only a small percentage of the whole iceberg is visible above the surface. In this way, the iceberg is like the mind. The conscious mind is what we notice above the surface, while the unconscious mind, the largest and most powerful part, remains unseen below the surface.

The unconscious mind holds all awareness that is not present in the conscious mind. All memories, feelings, and thoughts that are out of conscious awareness are, by definition, 'unconscious.' It is also called the subconscious and is known as the dreaming mind or deep mind.

There is tremendous power under the iceberg, your Subconscious mind. The conscious mind is constantly supported by unconscious resources. Just think of all the things you know how to do without conscious awareness. For instance, the unconscious mind regulates all the systems of the body and keeps them in harmony with each other. It controls heart rate, blood pressure, digestion, the endocrine system, and the nervous system, just to name a few of its natural, automatic duties.

The conscious mind, like the part of the iceberg above the surface, is a small portion of the whole being. The conscious mind is what we ordinarily think of when we say 'my mind.' Only seven bits of information, plus or minus two, can be held consciously at one time. Everything else we are thinking, feeling, or perceiving, along with all our memories, remains unconscious until called into consciousness or until rising spontaneously.

As part of the soul growth process, the subconscious mind needs to be re-programmed. This storehouse contains a lot of negative energies that need to be cleared. When one begins this journey, it will be a rabbit hole. There is no end to how deep and how far, and how long this can be. (If you have not entered this rabbit hole, good for you - Ignorance is bliss).

For any person on a growth trajectory, the subconscious mind is the final great frontier. There are numerous techniques to bridge your conscious awareness into the programming of your subconscious. One can spend a lifetime working on clearing oneself and still not be done; this is how vast our subconscious mind is.

Lastly, in your life, there will always be those who judge you. There will be those who judge you who don't have a clue who you are or what you are really about. There will be those who judge you who aren't living to their fullest potential themselves. And there will even be those who judge you that know you best just because they may envy your drive or the road that you are on toward success and happiness in your life. In the end, most people will judge you, so instead of worrying about what people think, do what life calls you to do. To carry the iceberg metaphor forward, each of us can be represented as an iceberg, with the larger part of ourselves deeply submerged. And there's a place in the depths where all of our icebergs come together, a place in the unconscious where we connect. The psychologist Carl Jung has named this realm the 'Collective Unconscious.' This is the area of the mind where all humanity shares experience and from where we draw on the archetypal energies and symbols that are common to us all.

Another even deeper level can be termed the 'Universal Unconscious,' where experiences beyond just humanity can also be accessed with a regression process. It is at this level that many 'core issues' begin and where their healing needs to be accomplished.

Depending on the nature of your DNOS journey and your purpose, you will be guided to where the action is needed. This starts with clearing negative subconscious energies and then working towards helping the Human species by clearing the "Collective Unconscious" negative programming.

A short expert from "The Superhero Code" book:

- Scientists agree there are broadly two parts to

the mind: the conscious and subconscious mind. The conscious mind contains all the thoughts, memories, feelings, and wishes of which we are aware at any given moment. The subconscious mind is a reservoir of feelings, thoughts, urges, and memories that are outside of our conscious awareness, such as feelings of pain, anxiety, or conflict.

- Characteristics of the conscious mind o Thinking mind, Educational Mind, Intellectual Mind, Ability to Choose, Accept or Reject, Create Idea or Origination

- The conscious mind is the gatekeeper and filters information that goes into the subconscious.

Clearing negative vibrations from your Conscious and Subconscious mind and enriching it with positive experiences that align with your Soul is your DNOS journey. This is your Metamorphosis.

DARK NIGHT OF THE SOUL VS. DEPRESSION

"There can be no rebirth without a Dark Night of the Soul, a total annihilation of all that you believed in and thought that you were." - Hazrat Inayat Khan.

T he "Dark Night of the Soul" is a specific brand of deep suffering. It is a concept that goes back hundreds of years in history. In the 16th century, poet and mystic Saint John of the Cross wrote about the Dark Night of the Soul in *La Noche Oscura Del Alma* and wrestled with discerning between depression and a Dark Night of the Soul. The symptoms are similar, but you will feel the difference in the depth of spiritual transformation that occurs.

The deep suffering associated with a Dark Night of the Soul is known by other terms in other disciplines. In Shamanism, this prolonged state is called "soul loss," or descent to the underworld. In Greek mythology, it is known as *katabasis*, and Carl Jung understood it symbolically in terms of alchemy as *nigredo*. Each reference is about a period of darkness where your soul is separated from God. During this split, your false self is wholly destroyed, and you are remade into your true self.

Most people who experience a night of the soul realize that nothing makes them happy anymore. They can no longer experience bodily or sexual pleasure, their emotions are dulled, and no joy comes from material possessions or even spiritual practice. This state of intense apathy is the beginning of the purification process, and it is another blessing in disguise.

This is easy enough to theorize about, but when you are going through it in reality, it is absolutely terrifying. The ground beneath your feet is ripped out from beneath you, and you are in the midst of great loss and suffering. Such are the trials of life. When it's happening, all you want is for it to stop. You do not immediately recognize that your suffering is a positive omen of change. It does not feel like that, but it is there to let you know that you can no longer continue to live the way you have been living.

We have been discussing the two things side by side all along without calling attention to the difference between suffering and a Dark Night of the Soul, and the two experiences do have important differences between them.

Not all suffering is as intense as a dark night. Not all suffering is about resolving imbalanced karmic energy. Sometimes, you just suffer hardship, and it's terrible, and you get through it, and not much else has changed.

With a Dark Night of the Soul, though, life is very intense for an extended time. Your core center is deeply unsatisfied as your whole being lives the experience of resolving karma. People move in and out of your life swiftly and with divine purpose and timing. Your soul is on the move as you suffer, as you are becoming a seeker of knowledge and spiritual wisdom. Burning desires grip you desperately and do not let you go. They remain there, burning inside of you until you resolve the obstacles and surrounding tension that has suffocated your desires for too long.

Not only are you on fire from the inside, but things burn away from the outside world as well when undergoing a Dark Night of the Soul. More than suffering a "bad day" or a "tough time" as you normally would, the spiritual casing that wraps the darkness also flavors this brand of suffering quite differently. You will lose complete interest in physical things; your mind will travel down complicated rabbit holes of discovery where you find there is so much more to learn.

The more you learn, the more you grow and evolve, the more your intuition comes online and your communication channels open, and the more your spirit awakens. When you are finally through it, you are not the same person you were when it began.

When you suffer, in general, you might reach a point of anger with God, but this fury is not attached to your suffering. With a Dark Night of the Soul, you are at war with God, demanding an end to your pain. In the beginning, you latch yourself onto a cycle of anger. You're angry with God; then you're angry with yourself; then you're angry at life. It just keeps going until you realize what is happening. Then, depending upon your purpose and where your soul is in its evolution, the darkness lasts until it clears.

As with any period of suffering, there is no good answer to the question of how long this will last. Take comfort in knowing your soul has a higher purpose —otherwise, you would not suffer this way. Take comfort in also knowing that you will be led to and through every node of growth along the way so that you are given a salve as you go through the suffering.

Some have defined this as a time of spiritual despair. You feel disconnected and empty. The emptiness is from feeling completely divided from God. It is a time of sadness, loss, and spiritual urgency. The darkness of the night is when your eyes are closed, and you must rely on other senses. Not only do you lose connection with God and feel devoid of all spirituality, but you feel betrayed by life itself and find yourself without a sure ground to walk upon. In the darkness of the night, your old life loses its meaning and falls away so that you can grow into a new version of yourself.

The term is misleading as it lasts much longer than a night. Just how long your suffering will last is unpredictable, but some have likened the terminology to what's known as a "polar night." This phenomenon occurs at the northernmost and southernmost poles of the Earth. Because of the tilt of the Earth's axis, the area inside these polar circles experiences a 'night' that lasts longer than 24 hours. As awful as the prolonged darkness seems, it holds astonishing potential because the opposite can also occur. The "polar day" happens when the sun is above the horizon for longer than 24 hours in the same areas of the Earth but at a different point in time. It makes sense to conceptualize 'day' and 'night' here as abstract and undefined seasons of time similar to your soul's suffering and the lasting fulfillment that comes with your freedom from suffering.

Many people liken this experience to the clinical diagnosis of depression. Conventionally, this is how people speak of their suffering: in terms of being depressed. In this state of impaired mental health, you feel there is no purpose to anything, and nothing makes sense anymore. However, a Dark Night of the Soul is a state of total impairment of health. This variety of suffering impacts your physical, mental, emotional, and spiritual health. The depression that you feel is real. It is part of your suffering, but it is not the totality of your suffering. You will feel what people with depression feel. You may want to withdraw from the world or remove yourself from it. These feelings are normal.

One important difference between depression and a Dark Night of the Soul is that depression can be treated with medication and therapy to the point of alleviating some or all of the mental health suffering. In short, you treat the two things differently. Depression is a likely part of your Dark Night of the Soul, but not everyone who is depressed is going through one. The source of depression is also different from the source of suffering during a Dark Night of the Soul. Depression is rooted in chemical imbalances in the body and self-sabotaging thought patterns and can result from illness, abuse, or genetics. In comparison, a dark night is rooted in your soul's existential crisis and can result from simply embarking upon your soul's journey.

Some sure signs will alert you to the fact that you're going through a Dark Night of the Soul rather than suffering from depression alone. If you can check all or most of these boxes, it might help you accept where you are on your soul's journey. Keep in mind that these are also symptoms of depression, so by themselves, they are not enough to differentiate between the two states of suffering. It's helpful to think of them as depression and dark night depression.

The first is a heavy feeling of sadness. It doesn't matter why you are in despair or what caused it; it only matters that you feel unhappy. The next clue is that on top of the sadness, you also feel unworthy. You are sure you do not deserve the happiness you lost, nor do you deserve anything remotely positive to enter your sphere. You don't deserve love, respect, success, attention, or to feel better. The persistent feeling of being doomed to a life of suffering is another sign of a dark night. The emptiness will feel eternal. In truth, all of the symptoms might feel eternal. Another dark night marker is feeling powerless to change your situation and hopeless that it will improve. Compound that with the fact that your self-control will be compromised, and it will be hard for you to take any kind of action. This is not to say that you can't or won't take action, but it will be difficult. It will also be challenging to find joy in the things you once loved or even the energy or drive to do them. The general feeling of craving will also persist, and you will long for comfort, but the comfort of your known world will be gone.

Taken together, these symptoms of depression synthesize into a dark night depression that is more philosophical than the usual melancholia. Another key distinction between depression and A Dark Night of the Soul is how the two brands of suffering end. When you come out of your depression, you are pretty much the same person you were: You still have your habits, thought patterns, and beliefs, and the only real difference is that you feel better—thankfully!

When your Dark Night of the Soul ends (and it will end eventually), your former life is unrecognizable. Little remains the same. Not only do you feel better and recategorize your life as an incredible experience, but you think better, relate better, and connect with God better.

How Dark Night of the Soul Manifests - Externally and Internally

"*The Dark Night of the Soul is when you have lost the flavor of life but have not yet gained the fullness of divinity. So it is that we must weather that dark time, the period of transformation when what is familiar has been taken away, and the new richness is not yet ours.*" – Ram Dass.

The great Indian art theorist and theologian Ananda Kumaraswamy said, "No creature can attain a higher grade of nature without ceasing to exist. In the dark night, something of your makeup comes to an end—your ego, yourself, your creativity, you're meaning. You may find in that darkness a key to your source, the larger soul that makes you who you are and holds the secrets of your existence."

We've already discussed how the Dark Night of the Soul (DNOS) differs from depression or general suffering. It's a spiritual reset that prompts metamorphoses. If you're in the midst of a dark night yourself, you're probably paying extra attention to your body and your emotions. You might notice that while your tank is empty, there is also a creative process unfolding within you. Although you may be suffering, the experience might be painful, but these manifestations are indications of progress. For example, on the outside, you may be depressed, lonely, or anxious. You may even suffer from regular headaches or fatigue. Perhaps you're under increased stress. These symptoms might seem like evidence that you're suffering, that you're deeply depressed, and that you must do something to turn your life around. But these symptoms aren't to be feared or shunned. They're simply indicators that you're undergoing a process, a rebirth that will leave you stronger and happier than before. (Beliefnet, 2022).

On an internal level, a similar process unfolds. Internally, you may have a deep longing or a general feeling of inadequacy. You may experience disappointment, worry, and misery. You may feel betrayed by loved ones or betrayed by the world. You may even experience bouts of anguish or sorrow. Through all of this, you'll probably discover that the previous attachments you held so dear are now meaningless. This is a sign that your ego is ready to transform. This process is difficult. It involves much anguish and heartache, but it's the precursor to life's greatest treasure. By understanding what to expect on both an internal and external level, you can lessen the anxiety that the dark night heralds. And instead, you can approach it with curiosity and understanding.

In this chapter, I will discuss both the internal and external symptoms which arise during a Dark Night of the Soul. And additionally, I will provide suggestions on how to lessen anxiety and make the most out of this period. I'll offer tips on how to experience your dark night through the most peaceful approach possible. Highs and lows are a natural part of life. No one wakes up happy every single day. We all must grapple with bad days and bad years. So, you're not alone in this. With that being said, we all know what it's like to experience rough periods. We know that there are ways to see the light, even when life seems especially dark. The experience of your Dark Night of the Soul doesn't have to be miserable. Darkness is inevitable, but through understanding the symptoms you're experiencing, you can apply meaning to them and even create a sense of hope for yourself. So, let's explore each of the external symptoms first...

Psychosomatic Issues

When we experience a Dark Night of the Soul, our bodies undergo a lot of physical stress. This is because our emotions and our physical bodies are intrinsically linked. One affects the other and vice versa. Most of us have heard this said before. When you get a bad headache, or you start breaking out in acne or rashes, your loved one may ask, "Do you think it could be stress?" More likely than not, the answer is yes, even if you don't realize it at the moment. Our emotions play a massive role in our overall physical well-being. When you're feeling good on the inside, you're probably feeling good in your body as well.

Dr. Susan Bell, a psychologist who specializes in trauma-induced depression, believes that when we suffer from stress or anxiety often, we debilitate our bones over an extended amount of time. She believes our muscles are restricted and stressed when our minds are stressed as well. When our bones are tense for too long, they enter a state of more permanent debilitation. This is why some people suffer from prolonged back pain or other physical pains. It's a message from the body saying, "I need to be free. I need to relax." A Dark Night of the Soul can prompt these feelings with frequent intensity.

Pain experts believe around 15-30% of patients reporting chronic pain have a history of Post-Traumatic Stress Disorder (PTSD). This makes sense since, as I stated previously, our bodies and our minds are intrinsically connected. Therefore, if you've endured prolonged abuse or mistreatment, your body will remember it. And when your mind is triggered once again, your body will react similarly. Scientists now have reason to believe that certain specific symptoms represent specific stressors. Let's explore what each of these is.

Headaches are said to be a result of the everyday stresses in our lives. Migraines, for example, maybe a sign that your everyday routine or practices are causing stress in your mind and body. If you find that you experience an excessive number of headaches during your Dark Night of the Soul, see if there's a way you can adjust your routine. Create more space for relaxation and activities that bring you peace and happiness. A change in routine could very well alleviate your head's pain.

If you're experiencing pain in your neck or throat, scientists believe that it may be a sign you have trouble with forgiveness. Essentially, it may be difficult for you to forgive those around you or even yourself. If you're holding on to grudges or you're carrying a lot of animosity toward the people in your life, your neck may feel the effects. Make sure that you aren't being too hard on yourself. Practice forgiveness and see if your neck and throat experience a release with your newfound grace.

If you carry a lot of pain in your shoulders, it could be a sign that you are metaphorically carrying the weight of the world on your back. Maybe you internalize the pain of others or try to save people without giving yourself the same patience and attention. In the same vein, pain in the upper back may suggest that you are craving love or emotional support in some way. Lower back pain reflects a similar issue, but it's more related to financial or worldly stress. There are also more acute pains that point to very specific internal hang-ups. For example, elbow pain is said to reflect resistance or fear of change. And if you experience pain in your palm, it could mean you find it hard to reach out to others for support. Perhaps you need to find the courage to lean on others more.

If you're experiencing pain in your hips, that could be a sign that you're afraid of forward momentum. Perhaps you want to move ahead in life, but you fear the results or what will happen in the process. Look out for hip pain, for it may be a reflection of your perceived, stunted progress. Alternatively, if you suffer from chronic knee pain, it may be a sign that your ego needs a rebirth— which is especially common during the Dark Night of the Soul. And if you suffer from liver problems, it could mean that you have an unhealthy relationship with anger. Similarly, issues with the lungs may reveal unexpressed or unacknowledged grief. Heart and brain issues may reflect problems with too much worrying, and kidney problems are reportedly a result of too much fear.

No matter what physical ailment you may be suffering from, there is research that points to a specific mental root. It may be wise to search the internet for what kind of mental stressors may be affecting your physical body. That way, you can get to the source of the issue and figure out what it says about your soul's journey as well. If you're experiencing increased back pain during your Dark Night of the Soul, for example, your soul's journey may have themes of self-love and acquiring the love that you deserve. The mind, body, and spirit are all connected. We tend to become more aware of this during the Dark Night of the Soul. Davis (2022).

So, once you understand the source of your symptoms, once you know the root and understand why stress or depression has wreaked havoc on your psyche, what can you do to alleviate the pain? What are the steps you can take to restore peace in your mind and body? The good news is there are several ways you can restore internal harmony, practices that you can start implementing today to gain some stability and solace amidst the chaos. The first involves creating a strong life philosophy for yourself.

Life philosophies give us a framework to rely on. They put our primary values into focus and ensure that we always have principles to lean on when everything else in life grows blurry or confusing. Our values take on new importance during the dark nights of the soul. This is because our egos and previous attachments go through a dissolving period. The Dark Night of the Soul usually begins with some form of loss. We lose those things which we previously depended on for safety and security, and we're challenged to redefine ourselves according to new structures. This requires a reassessment of core values. If we previously put a lot of value on financial stability, for example, then the DNOS brings a loss of a loved one, we may decide that money is not as important as time with friends and family. You may shift your values according to this newfound wisdom.

Our values form the foundation of our life philosophies. My Dark Night of the Soul led me to reconsider my values in a major way, which also resulted in a new life philosophy. At the start of my DNOS, my partner left for Spain to go to grad school. My roommate and my best friend also moved to grad school in the same year, and I was suddenly isolated. These were the people I spent all my time with, and just like that, they were gone. Their absence left an emptiness in its wake. I realized that I had invested too much of my security and happiness into my relationships with others. Once they were gone, I had little of my own life to fall back on. I relied on them for fun, social fulfillment, artistic inspiration, financial security, and many more facets of my life. Suddenly, I was challenged to take charge of my happiness. I couldn't rely on others to provide it for me. At the same time, I learned that I had to embrace change. I had to be okay with the fact that some people wouldn't stay in my life forever, and that's okay.

This led me to a total shift in personal values. Before my Dark Night of the Soul, I was obsessed with marriage. I'd panic if anyone close to me even suggested taking an extended vacation or leaving me alone for too long. But with my loved ones' absence, I realized that I value my freedom a lot. I discovered that I could work remotely and travel to visit all of my friends without being obsessed with roots or stability. I found myself again through traveling and dating casually—this time, without all the hang-ups about marriage and the future. I discovered that if I just lived in the present, I could enjoy life and relish in the now. I don't have to care what happens in the future, I decided. And that changed everything for me. These are the kinds of revelations that dark nights of the soul promise. They give us a rich opportunity to realign our values from a more evolved state of mind.

We all need a life philosophy because philosophies provide meaning. They point to a personal truth that quiets all the chaos and grounds us when everything else is upside down. Without a philosophy of life, you may be swamped by your emotions and believe that life is meaningless. You see the chaos in and around you, and you assume that it could never make sense. With this attitude, it is easy to latch onto simplistic explanations, which are never far away.

Your life philosophy should be personal to you and your values. It shouldn't reflect the life philosophy of anyone else. It needs to come from your intuition. It may take some time before you fully embody your new philosophy, and that's okay. You can't rush the process, but take your time and be honest with yourself. Realize that the DNOS heralds a transformation. You may be surprised that you want things that are completely different from what you wanted before. But that's natural! You're not the same person you were before. So, experience all of your emotions, consider what you've learned through your dark night, and then reassess your values. With your new life philosophy, life will never be as scary as it was before your DNOS.

Dark Night of the Soul is Your Metamorphosis

"The Dark Night of the Soul is a journey into light, a journey from your darkness into the strength and hidden resources of your soul." – Caroline Myss.

The Dark Night of the Soul is an essential rite of passage. Although it often seems devastating, it is an essential part of the soul's growth. In order to grow, we have to transform. We must shed our old skin to be reborn anew. That's why the Dark Night of the Soul is so significant. It marks a critical point in the soul's development. Without it, we wouldn't grow, and we'd only have the opportunity to experience life on a surface level. It also marks a critical point in our ego development because the ego's desires are usually at odds with the soul's needs. This is the basis of the DNOS struggle. The ego wants one thing, while the soul needs something else.

Everyone experiences a period in their lives when they realize that something is missing. It often occurs, most glaringly, in the late twenties or early thirties when many ego goals are completed, but a new sense of emptiness settles in. An ego death and transformation must occur in order to evolve on a soul level. Our souls don't come into physical incarnation already fully formed— they arrive with a purpose and a specific goal. Our souls must endure karmic tests and challenges; they must find enrichment through different experiences and, through those experiences, discover what the soul truly desires. At the moment of ego transformation, there is often a loss of desire. The things that once offered a sense of fun and joy suddenly lack meaning. But this lays the groundwork for new insights. When life lacks meaning, the ego is malleable. It has room to shift its form and find new attachments that center around the soul's needs.

There are many reasons why it takes years for the soul's needs to find a voice. Societal expectations and expectations from family or friends can form the basis for ego attachments that don't necessarily align with the soul. This is why the Dark Night of the Soul is like a self-created mess. It's a moment when past decisions may come back to haunt you, but that's only because the universe is pushing you toward something better, something more meaningful and right. You may find that your life is full of obstacles on your dark night and that no matter how hard you try, setbacks keep arising. However, this is just a sign from the universe that you must go with the flow and see where your soul wants to take you. When the voice of the ego is muted, the sounds of the soul can rise to the surface.

Additionally, there's also a reason why the Dark Night of the Soul leaves us empty. There's the old cliche that to create room for the "new," we have to let go of the "old." This is essentially what the Dark Night of the Soul is doing. It starts with a loss in one form or another and culminates with a new foundation. Usually, the loss is trying to tell us something. It's meant to redirect our values in some way. If you lose all your money, it may be a sign that you need to reorient your relationship with money, for example. If you lose a loved one, it may be a nudge from the universe that you should put less emphasis on others and make yourself a priority instead. It could also be a reminder that you've been too focused on shallow things. This is the plot of many movies. The protagonist loses their spouse because they've been too focused on work, and suddenly, they realize it's love that they truly desire. By the end of the movie, the character is changed, but only because their values have changed. They're not the same person they were in the first ten minutes of the film. They have new priorities now. They've made it through the Dark Night of the Soul, and they've found the soul's elixir waiting on the other side.

Unfortunately, the struggle is an inherent part of the metamorphosis. It is often only when things are really difficult and we're presented with truly challenging life circumstances that we have enough push to make a radical change. Things fall apart so we can create something new. It happens in nature every day, so why would our human existence and destinies function any differently? But there are a few factors that determine the length and depth of our struggles. For instance, if we resist change rather than flow with it, we may find that the struggle lasts longer.

If we react to the dark night by trying desperately to control everything, we will only make the process worse. Let's say you lost your job, and you feel very conflicted about this. On the one hand, you might realize that you didn't like the job that much, anyway. Maybe there's a brief flicker in your mind which says I *could finally pursue my passion for painting*. But as weeks go by and your bank account dwindles, you rush to find whatever job is similar to your last one. You repress the quiet yearning of your soul so that you can control the chaos life is throwing you. This may work on a surface level.

You may be comforted temporarily. But as years go by, your soul begins to decay... metaphorically speaking. That's the thing with the soul. Its nudges never go away. It needs to grow and evolve. If you temporarily shush it, its voice will only grow louder. And your next Dark Night of the Soul experience could be much more stressful. It's better to face your fears head-on than let them ruminate inside you. That's how chronic illness occurs. So, understand that struggle is inevitable, but you can lessen the anxiety and the pain by facing the struggle directly.

Depending on your purpose, there's a high chance that your deepest desires are tied directly to your Dark Night of the Soul. When the dark night arrives, the soul can reveal more than just cravings and clues to a deeper, truer identity; it also reveals purpose. Sometimes, this purpose arrives in the form of a person. It could be a new partner, child, or spouse who opens your mind and inspires you toward a new path in life. It could arrive as an opportunity, such as a new job or responsibility. You might want to pursue something new, and in the midst of that, the people in your life may feel confused or threatened. Often, a Dark Night of the Soul coincides with a period of dysfunction in personal relationships because self-discovery involves confusion on all accounts. It also involves some changes in identity, so when you're in the throes of a Dark Night of the Soul, you may experience some separation and difficulty in your personal relationships. It's only natural that when we change, so do our relationships. But this is an opportunity to form more authentic and soulful connections.

If your destiny doesn't arrive in the form of a new relationship, it may arrive in a reawakened passion or a sudden epiphany that reveals your true vocation. You may take a new job, thinking that it's just a temporary day job, only to discover you have a passion for whatever niche industry you're now immersed in. The experience could catapult you into a new lifelong obsession and sense of fulfillment. What once seemed like a horrible ending is now a beautiful new opportunity. These are the kinds of experiences the Dark Night of the Soul promises. And this is why it's best to approach the dark night with curiosity rather than fear. At any moment, a light can appear in the depths of the fog. It could be a sudden illumination, a moment of inspiration, or a chance to meet with someone or something that lights your soul on fire. The more you are clear with yourself and your desires at a subconscious level, the easier it is to welcome these experiences with positivity.

Psychologist, Robert Puff, believes that our mindset is a huge factor in determining how we cope with major changes and life transitions. He states,

"When big things happen, we tend to think, 'I have a right to be upset.' And it's true—terrible things that happen to us will most likely make us upset—but at the same time, our thoughts create our reality. If we associate experiencing something upsetting with needing to feel unhappy now, perhaps for longer, then this is going to be our reality. No matter the situation, I can almost guarantee you that someone else has gone through the same thing, and they are doing absolutely fine." (Puff, 2021).

Puff, like most psychologists, believes that it is our attitude, more than anything, which determines our happiness or our unhappiness. So, we are so lucky that we have knowledge about the Dark Night of the Soul. We have examples to study, both in real life and in the fictional stories we consume daily. We can ease our anxieties through the knowledge that darkness is essential. It leads to progress. With this mindset, we can take control of our dark night in a way that doesn't involve gripping old-life structures. We can find peace by letting go and growing curious.

We always have the ability to reframe our thoughts. So instead of thinking, 'Wow, my life is falling apart. What did I do to deserve this?' we can think, 'Wow, life as I knew it is no longer. What is my soul preparing for me now? What do I want to do with this new freedom?' It's easier to operate from a place of positivity with this new, more optimistic outlook. Curiosity is your best friend when it comes to any major life transition. You might wonder what the caterpillar thinks as it prepares to transition into its cocoon. Is it terrified? Is it worried about the future? Or does it enter its next phase with excitement? Maybe it wonders what colors or patterns will appear on its wings. More than likely, the caterpillar doesn't have the brain capacity to ponder such questions. But even so, it's useful to think about what we gain from worrying.

By now, you probably know the answer... there's very little to gain from any form of fear, especially when it comes to the Dark Night of the Soul. We can't predict how our own metamorphosis will transpire, but we can let go and give in to the mystery of the universe. We can choose to trust our souls, which is both the scariest and most exciting thing you can do as a human. If nothing else, choose to give in to the human experience. Otherwise, what's the point of even living?

THE DARK NIGHT OF THE SOUL JOURNEY–WHAT TO EXPECT

"Dark Night of the Soul is not merely "having a bad day" or even a week. The Dark Night is a long, pervasive, and very dark experience. If you're experiencing the Dark Night of the Soul, you will constantly carry around within you a sense of being lost. Your Heart will constantly, in some shape or form, be in mourning, and this is because you long deep down to feel the presence of your Soul again." – Aletheia Luna.

Some people live their whole life buying into the conventions of modern society. They live life on autopilot, allowing their ego-self to make decisions and take action. Their life is habitual and based on their internalized conditioning from the surrounding social and cultural environment.

Other people are rudely awakened from this state of unconsciousness. Often, a personal tragedy will send these people into deep suffering where their faith wanes as they lose all sense of their former selves in the process of becoming spiritually advanced versions of their highest selves. Something shakes them from their daily, narrow view of life and catapults them into the darkness to be transformed.

There are several inevitabilities on the journey through the Dark Night of the Soul. For one, life gets very intense. Usually, there is some form of loss or separation, which serves as the catalyst for resolving karma. When all of your ego structures fall and shatter, there's no choice but to build yourself back again. It's a painful and often grueling process, but it's also the means to greater clarity and authenticity. It offers the path toward true fulfillment. But the process of loss and re-identification is intense. It often feels like a sort of death, like you're forced to start at ground zero once more. The core of who you are will feel profoundly unsatisfied, and people may come and go as you learn who you are all over again. Life may slow down at first but then pick up speed soon afterward as your soul rushes to move around and achieve progress. You will suddenly become a seeker on a quest for spiritual truths. And through that quest, you will discover parts of yourself you didn't know existed. This is where the healing begins...

Through the process of rediscovery, you'll find that many beliefs you once held were rooted in fears, traumas, and internalized false negatives. For example, the Dark Night of the Soul usually heralds an epiphany, in which a person realizes that a certain self-belief is not their belief but the belief of their family, friends, or partners. When I experienced my Dark Night of the Soul, I was very critical of myself. After the failure of a co-dependent relationship, I thought there was something wrong with me. I thought that I wasn't successful enough because my parents never told me they were proud of me. I thought that I was too sensitive because I was never allowed to show emotion as a child—feelings were swept under the rug in my home, never to be discussed. All of this created a false narrative within me. For years, I held on to the belief that I was somehow inferior. On a conscious level, I thought that I deserved things like love, success, and happiness. But on a subconscious level, some part of me considered that I wasn't worthy.

When my relationship ended and my best friends moved to a different state for grad school, I was all alone. So, I had to redefine myself and learn how to be self-sufficient. It was no longer acceptable for me to seek happiness through external sources such as other people or personal achievements. I needed to find it from within. This was difficult because I had never done it before, but I knew there was a reason for this. I knew that through the tunnel of struggle, I would find a light that didn't flicker or wane... a permanent glow. So instead of following my friends to a new state, I got my apartment and began the difficult process of building a new life. That's when I discovered my true vocation of healing and life coaching. It was also when I met the love of my life.

The whole experience was terrifying. I was in the unknown, lonely and afraid. But through building something from square one, I learned that many of the beliefs about myself I had held from childhood were false. Through meeting a partner who appreciated my sensitivities, I learned that I wasn't too sensitive. Through discovering my passion for healing, I learned that I wasn't a failure by society's standards. I just simply hadn't found my niche. And through falling in love again and making myself vulnerable, I learned that I was worthy of happiness and abundance. There wasn't anything wrong with me. I was simply wrong for holding onto negative beliefs. Now, I am forever changed. I'll never be the person I was before my Dark Night of the Soul. Now, I live through my soul's purpose and find endless energy and motivation through its life-giving sustenance. My life is very different, but it also has a new meaning. It's different in a good way. The experience left me whole and healed.

These are the things you can expect to experience during your own Dark Night of the Soul. As you lose grip on the things that previously framed your ego identity, you will find new burning desires within you. You will find a new spiritual appreciation for life, and the voice of your intuition will gain volume as you can't help but hear and respond to its nudges. Once you hear the whispers from your intuition and you begin the process of reorienting your life based on those nudges, you are ready to walk into the light. It's impossible to say how long your journey with the Dark Night of the Soul will take. For some people, it may last a few months. For others, it may last several years.

More likely than not, it will arrive as a gradual process. One significant change may set the whole process in motion, but the struggles and resulting revelations could crop up for several years in sudden bursts.

The length of your dark night may also depend on your specific purpose. If your true purpose requires more tests and challenges to build you up, then your path through the darkness may be longer, but the light at the end of the tunnel will be richer and brighter as well. Some of us require more of a struggle to get to our final destination, and that's okay. Remember, your soul chose your path for a reason. Deep down, you know that you must endure and that you will survive. You'll not only survive but thrive in a new form. Additionally, depending on how evolved your soul is in your current incarnation, you may not need a long dark night. If you're already fairly evolved on a soul level, you may be able to pick up the pieces of your life and listen to your intuition when it first makes its presence known. After that, you can work toward making your life what you want it to be, and the darkness will dissipate with each step toward progress.

Sometimes, the length of your dark night journey is dependent upon other puzzle pieces that are waiting to fall into place. It could be you're meant to meet a soulmate or some other significant guide, but so long as you hesitate to go out into the world, your progress is stunted. Sometimes your soul must wait for another soul to meet you on your path. And this will no doubt affect the timing of your own dark night. Remember that your soul cluster is like an intricate web. It relies on precise timing to offer fated encounters that may change the course of your life. And sometimes, your dark night may include bursts of light.

You may meet your soulmate while you're still working on finding your purpose. This helps to lessen the anxiety of the whole experience. Just because a Dark Night of the Soul is dark doesn't mean that it has to be entirely painful. We all experience difficult months or years, but within those periods, we also have moments of hope, amusement, or light. So even if your dark night ends up lasting longer than the average person's, it's not all bad. You may just need more time to access the abundance of light within you.

In extreme cases, you may experience harsh lows during your dark night cycle. These are all extremes, but some people endure difficult situations such as suicidal thoughts, a lack of inner peace, dullness in life, or a period of extreme introversion. As previously mentioned, some people lose their friends, parents, or spouses. Sometimes, people have sleepless nights and find that their mental, emotional, or physical health is damaged. Other times, a new physical ailment arises that leads to feelings of insecurity.

You may lose your faith in God or any form of a higher power. And all of this could lead to anger directed at yourself or your life. While each of these situations is difficult and even traumatizing, it's important to remember that there is a deeper meaning and purpose to such events. Sometimes it's our greatest suffering that produces our greatest gifts. Through that awareness, you can embrace difficult periods as a lesson and a means toward evolved growth. Suffering brings growth, a chance for healing, and a creative opportunity to discover personal strength. If you fall into one of these extreme cases, don't worry. There is always a light at the end of the tunnel. Remember that the

Dark Night of the Soul is a rite of passage, and you will come out the other side healed and metamorphosed.

The Dark Night of the Soul can be broken down into seven specific stages. First, there is the moment when you wake up to the truth. This falls closely in line with a triggering event or even several triggering events. Then comes the fall to rock bottom— the period of loss and decay. Next is the chaos of major ups and downs, followed by a renewed sense of purpose. Then, with a new sense of balance and stability, you can transform into the very best version of yourself. This is generally the timeline for the Dark Night of the Soul, and each step is an important milestone toward meaning and wholeness. You can't skip one to fast-forward to the next. Each step serves a purpose that provides wisdom and truth. So, let's explore each of these steps more thoroughly...

It's no surprise that the first step on the dark night journey involves waking up to the truth. You suddenly realize that the old things you attributed so much meaning to are no longer meaningful. It's like a punch in your gut that indicates, 'I need a new source of meaning.' Life becomes dull and purposeless. This sensation may arrive at the onset of loss, or it may take some time before it settles in. But once the feeling arrives, there is no denying it. It's an emptiness that begs the soul to transform and shapeshift. Once you accept the truth that life needs new meaning, that your ego must die and be reborn again, then you're ready to accept the Dark Night of the Soul as your essential rite of passage. You can begin the critical journey.

Afterward, you may experience a triggering event or, perhaps, multiple triggering events, which further illuminate the need for greater meaning. The context and substance of these events will differ for every person, but generally, they bring loss in some form. You may lose your job after losing a partner or loved one. Your friends may move away, or a parent may pass away. There are a wide variety of events that may trigger the stereotypical dark night depression. However, these events are heralding something new. They're meant to shake the foundation of your life so new flowers can emerge through the cracks. To gain, we also have to sacrifice. So, while it may seem as though the world is delivering a cruel and dark fate, this is just an essential turning point. The universe is decluttering, so you have room for something new. It may appear tragic because the Dark Night of the Soul usually promises several difficult events. There may be the initial event that wakes you up to the truth, but the following event plummets you into the next phase... the darkness of the underworld.

The darkest time arrives at the third stage of the soul's progression. This is because all the major incidents have already occurred, and you have time and space to mourn but also reflect on what's missing. Through grieving whatever has slipped away, you realize what matters most to you. If you lost a significant partner, for example, you need time to mourn the relationship and identify why it mattered to you so much. Once you've fully allowed yourself to experience the emotions and feel the weight of the loss, you can begin the process of healing and looking forward. You can look to the future with curiosity and see that amid all the chaos, there is also excitement. The universe is preparing you for something. Anything can happen at any moment, and while depression may still linger, there is also hope and a sense of openness.

After hitting "rock bottom," there is usually a sort of rollercoaster effect. You may experience moments of pure bliss and joy followed by prolonged phases of stress, anxiety, or depression. You may have good days followed by bad days as you try to navigate what makes you happy while you're running on empty. This is a difficult period, but a necessary one, nonetheless. You need this time to experience the highs and lows before you're ready to discover a deeper meaning. Before we can devote ourselves to something, we need to know what it means to be truly alive. Sometimes, being alive is a chaotic experience. This period can make it feel as though you're going crazy. You may be jumping for joy one minute and crying the next. But these are the kinds of experiences you need to achieve balance and stability once more. It's like the pendulum, which swings back and forth before landing in the center. You need to give yourself time to live after feeling the effects of rock bottom. (Boomer, 2020).

DARK NIGHT OF THE SOUL –
REVEALING INNER BEAUTY

"*Every spiritual teaching points to the possibility of the end of suffering. Now, it is true that most teachers have had to go through the "Dark Night of the Soul," although for one or two it was very, very quick.*" – Eckhart Tolle.

R emember that our souls made a choice, or several choices, before incarnating into physical existence here on earth. These choices are unique to each soul and each individual, but the weight of your dark night may have a direct correlation to the unique mission your soul chose in this lifetime. So, what is the bigger picture? Why do some souls suffer longer than others? Some individuals may experience just a brief Dark Night of the Soul, lasting two or three short years. Others, however, suffer for decades. They go to prison, get lost in darkness, or suffer through prolonged persecution. This may seem unfair on the surface. But the length and tone of each dark night reveal something about the end goal.

We all welcome, on a subconscious level, the suffering that is required to achieve our greater purpose. If your dark night is especially long and gruesome, the light at the end of the tunnel may be especially bright as well. You may need to acquire more power and strength than the average person to achieve what you are meant to achieve. There are a few real-life examples of this kind of suffering, which preceded an acquired strength that changed the world.

Abraham Lincoln is a prime example of a person who had an especially grueling period of darkness, followed by a life-changing period of success, truth, and fulfillment. The majority of his childhood and early life was fraught with death, depression, and isolation, but this period also gave him strength and determination. Additionally, he acquired profound wisdom, which certainly helped when it came to leading a country of people.

Thomas Moore, an author of the Kosmos Journal for Global Transformation, believes that Lincoln may have sought leadership due to the specific challenges he dealt with growing up. He states,

"One outstanding example is Abraham Lincoln. With his early life surrounded by death and loneliness and his adult life weighed down by a war in which thousands of young men died, he was a seriously melancholic man who, in spite of his dark night, became an icon of wisdom and leadership. One theory is that he escaped his melancholy in his efforts for his country, but another possibility is that the very darkness of his life—he once said, 'If there's a worse place than hell, I'm in it.'—was the ground out of which his leadership grew." (Moore, 2020).

Nelson Mandela is another striking example of an influential person in history who had to enter the darkness before he was able to offer light to others. For a huge chunk of his life, Mandela was in prison—twenty-seven years, to be exact. Throughout all of those years, he lived under strict authority with no freedom under horrible conditions, and yet, he maintained his faith and saw the light at the end of the tunnel. Other prisoners have reported that he spent his nights doing sit-ups when he couldn't sleep. He didn't get into fights or curse the universe for his cruel fate. He understood that this horrible period in his life could act as the catalyst for something powerful in the future. And that's exactly what happened. Through the darkness, Mandela found the strength to lead as a powerful and prolific leader. He understood, first-hand, all the nuances of life's injustices. He saw that there was a lack of equality and freedom while he was in prison, and through that experience, he had the wisdom and strength to make a difference when he finally got out.

Additionally, there is a story in the bible, in the book of Corinthians, where Paul is afflicted by a thorn in his flesh, and he pleads with God to remove it. According to the

Bible, he did this at least three times, but God wouldn't remove it because doing so would eradicate the lesson that Paul was meant to learn, the lesson of grace. In the passage, God stated, "My grace is sufficient for you, for my power is made perfect in weakness." Later, in Romans, Paul utters the sentiment that neither "height nor depth" can "separate us from the love of God in Christ." So, you see how there's a symbolic suggestion here. Paul's story illuminates something about the soul's journey and purpose. His story suggests something about the way our human suffering not only humbles us but also fuels us. The statement about power being made perfect in weakness is especially profound, given our understanding of the soul's journey.

We need our weaknesses to discover our strengths. When we are in the midst of a Dark Night of the Soul, we become very aware of our weaknesses. It is typically a period when our self-esteem and confidence are at an all-time low. But the goal is not to do away with our weaknesses completely, but rather to look for God's grace in the midst of it. Sometimes it is the reflection on our weaknesses that motivates a new career or life direction. You may decide to become a wounded healer, for example. In that way, you alchemize the wound into a gift that can guide others. We can't plead our wounds and weaknesses away, but we can allow them to make us whole. We can grant them the ability to give us strength, and we can use that strength to make a difference in the world. That is the lesson of Paul's thorn.

A similar theme comes to the surface when you explore the story of Christ. On the one hand, the story of Jesus is tragic. Bursting with compassion and understanding, Jesus made it his sole mission to spread love and lead by example. He healed through love and inspired a nation by preaching his God-given wisdom. But in the end, he was crucified for his pursuits. He was forced to suffer and even die by the very people he was trying to save. But following his death, he was resurrected, which reveals something about the human soul. Sometimes a part of us needs to die to live out our mission with renewed power. Without Christ's resurrection, there would be no glory. This reveals something about our crosses that we all must bear. If your ego-self does not die, there is no space for a metamorphosis. And without metamorphosis, there is no growth. No evolution. (Ortlund, 2021).

It can be difficult to stay in tune with our divine natures when everything is going right or according to plan. It's easy to take things for granted or lose sight of the truth at these junctures. But when the chips are low, our egos are ripe for molding. It's easier to surrender to a higher purpose because all of our previous attachments are lost or given new meaning. This can provide comfort if you are in the middle of your fulfillment despite the Bible's dark Night of the soul. Suffering serves a purpose, and it acts as the necessary precursor to life's bounty and gold. Jesus knew this. Paul knew this. And many others learned through the process of their own dark nights. So long as you can find grace amidst the struggle, you'll emerge anew. You'll have more strength and more certainty than ever before.

THE CASE OF THE RED PILL

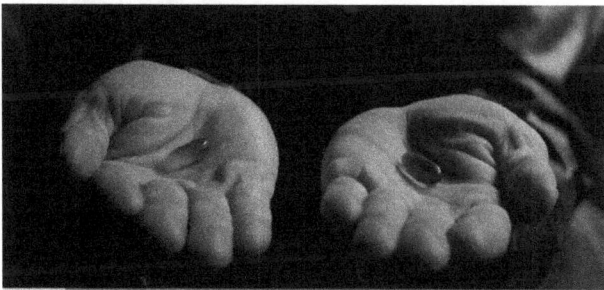

"The greatest miracles aren't seen in the calm, peaceful waters. They are seen in the rocky, turbulent, and frightful waters of a faith-filled life." –Kelly Balarie.

Whether you know your life's purpose already or not, your destiny awaits to magnetize you to your soul's calling.

Come with me on a metaphor.

Your soul's journey begins when you take the Red Pill. Symbolically, this means that on some level of your being, you have chosen to undergo a transformative process to be of service to the world in your fullest capacity.

Take heart. You are entering into deep, dark waters that swirl and threaten to pull you under. The experience will most likely be quite different than what you anticipate. Only the rare, brave souls are called onto this journey. Many of them have been preparing for many lifetimes to build up their courage. Believe that the wait is worth it and that you're ready, then dive right in.

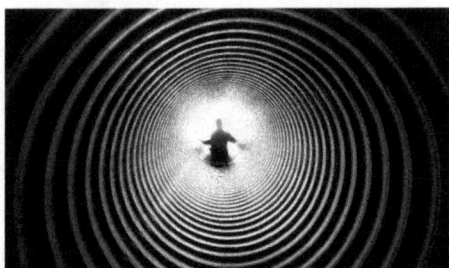

Once you embark on this journey, you will soon find that you are traveling out of your body. It happens often and immediately after you fall asleep. The journey that your soul is on is taking you out beyond this dimension and into the heavenly realms. You will find yourself engaged in many different projects and a multitude of experiences. You will also come to know your many guides, teachers, and muses along the way who come and go as you progress through your journey. It all happens there—in the heavenly realms, where you are trained to become the best version of yourself.

There is no way to know how long this journey lasts. It can be very challenging, and depending upon your soul's blueprint for your lifetime, your training could last for years, decades, or longer. If you know and surrender to the path your soul has called you to, then enduring the process will be easier. Keep going. Each new challenge is another opportunity to develop your awareness, and as you grow in spiritual awareness, your ability to traverse the higher realms and take back information from your travels increases.

Here is how the process unfolds.

Keep in mind that the following information is subjective, and not every person goes through all of the emotions discussed here. Again, what you experience depends on what your soul's purpose is, what your destiny holds, and what you are called to do in service to humanity, the galaxy, and creation itself.

The process requires an immense amount of physical energy and perseverance. From what I've gathered in my studies, it usually begins somewhere between the ages of your mid-twenties to your late thirties. In the early stages, you will experience a lot of excitement for life anew. Your capacity to learn is exponential. You come into contact with an abundance of new information, new people, and a new awareness that starts to kick in. You feel it working *in* you, in your thought processes and ability to focus, and you feel it working *on* you as if to grow you toward your best self. You work enthusiastically, and you become a seeker of knowledge, problems, and solutions. You might even find yourself doing a lot of research, gathering your information, exchanging ideas with friends, and asking thoughtful and thought-provoking questions of yourself and others.

You will find your higher communication channels start to open. It's the way that Source communicates with you. This is different for everyone. It can come through channels of intuition, imagination, deep listening, visions, dreams, gut feelings, and physical sensations. For me, the primary channels of communication are dreams, listening, and physical sensations in my body.

Soul Mates

As you make progress on your soul's journey, you will probably be introduced to other souls with whom you can choose to partner with for a greater purpose. Both of your souls then go through a transformation process to be compatible with each other so that together, they can make greater things happen. This kind of relationship is the literal meaning of a "match made in Heaven." Your two souls transform into harmony with each other, and your union, for however long it remains, allows you both to serve a greater purpose and service to society.

These matches are made in Heaven, though they may or may not manifest in the physical realm. It is very important that you know this; otherwise, you might spend your entire lifetime in waiting mode, wondering when something will happen, and nothing might ever happen. My advice to you is to not keep waiting for Heaven to make the first move. You can take charge. Sometimes, you must take control to make things happen.

Give yourself permission to be this powerful. From the higher perspective that watches any two soul mates journey together, it is observable that there are times when one soul is ready for more, but the other is not. That is okay. Still, it is the source of great pain and heartache, for a lot of emotions are involved. Your heart may be pierced so badly that you wish you could force things to be different. You cannot. However, if your soul mate does show up in the physical world, then it is the sweetest thing that you can ever experience. You will know joy and ecstasy for that time of your life.

Darkness Settles In

When the Dark Night comes to transform you, every belief pattern that you hold will be challenged. The things that you hold dearly may be lost, and your dreams might crumble as you lose things that once held value. Your entire life will be laid bare. In a way, you, as you once were, will be gone.

Your mind turns hyperactive, and you become more introverted as you think about everything that comes up. You are still in your physical body, but your awareness is not—most of your mind and consciousness will be elsewhere in the world. You may be physically present, but people will intuitively sense that you are mentally absent.

Make no mistake; your heart will be pierced, and you will be left longing for happiness. Your tears will seem endless. Your mental agony will be great. You might even develop migraines or other physical ailments during this time.

Very few people can relate to your suffering at this level, and no one will understand the reasons behind your depression. Any remedies you encounter will be short-lived. Your relationships may also be short-lived. Your parents, teachers, or priests will have no sufficient answers. The only other human beings who can truly understand and know your place in this process are other enlightened beings or perhaps your spiritual guru. For that reason, you might be drawn to these people on this journey.

Many times, you will wish that this path had not chosen you. You will wish for your blissful ignorance, but in the end, this path is the choice that a higher part of you made. Like in the movie, *The Matrix*, when the Oracle says to Neo, "You have already made the choice." Your journey will help you understand why so that you can make the best of it. The only thing you have in the Dark Night of the Soul is your faith and trust in a higher power and yourself.

A fire burns deep in your soul, a flame that does not extinguish even during the most difficult circumstances. This is your faith, and it is the only thing that will lead you through your soul's suffering. Yes, your faith will flicker. Yes, you will lose it time and again, but you will also recover it every time. This happens cyclically as you transform.

You will go through multiple phases of "ego deaths" that shed your old ways of being, too. Your heart will be pierced multiple times.

Warrior of Light Training

There are different types of soul journeys, and your unique training and simulations are directed accordingly. Let us briefly introduce the topic of a Soul Warrior journey. Forget any visual concept of "warrior" that you may have, for this spiritual archetype is in no way related to your physical body or gender identity. In the real world, you might be a weak, feeble-bodied person. In the higher realms where your soul calls to you, however, you may be a great and powerful warrior of light.

Your soul's journey could be the hardest thing you ever do, and it could take the longest amount of time to come to an end. Heroes are not made in a day. Behind every hero is a life story. This is true for real, everyday heroes in the world, and it is true for Superhero characters in popular culture. They mimic real heroes. A real hero is anyone who has ever had a positive influence on another person or place. Anyone who has a story of enduring the journey from darkness to light.

Soul journeys usually involve blood, toil, and suffering. They invoke the most difficult scenarios to traverse, and a warrior of light's mindset must be strong and sure. This attitude is more than what you might compare to being a "tree hugger" (which is a wonderful practice, by the way). A warrior of light is not just a loving, kind person. They are also a person of righteous anger when the situation demands it.

Their mind is strong, and their heart is stronger. A warrior of light is not hardened by the world and its criticisms. Their heart is open and ready to be shaped into their best form. If it needs to change, it will. This is the warrior's spiritual discipline.

Through consistent training, the warrior is humbled in spirit and heartened to continue the journey. They are rewarded for their efforts with a conscious awareness of their thought patterns. They grow in self-knowledge. They see their fear-based patterns of thinking that have been trapped in the conscious and subconscious. They need to be released and reprogrammed. The warrior's mind recognizes that this is where they are on their journey, and their heart finds the strength to stand in the middle of their fears and deconstruct the old version of themselves. It is natural to want to know how exactly this will unfold, but the truth is that it looks different for everyone. Your metaphorical battle with the darkness will unfold in your own unique manifestation of reality.

This warrior training is increasingly given to human beings on Earth at this time. These souls are a necessity for the world.

These topics are very depressing, dark, and deathly. Remember, for resurrection to happen, death is a prerequisite. Death is a must. Without death, there is no resurrection. Resurrection is the goal. With your rebirth comes great power, and that power comes with great responsibility.

Dreams and Visions

Pay attention to your dreams. Pay attention to your visions. Pay attention to your intuition and gut feelings. Your body and mind speak to you in abstract ways. You might see a symbol in your dream that prompts you to do some research and begin to understand the language of your dreams. Or you may receive a medical diagnosis that causes you to question the nature of healing and your body's sovereignty.

Dreams are the windows to your soul. The more you pay attention to your dreams, the more your dreams will come. Once you develop your intuition and the ability to analyze them, a new world of possibilities will open to you. You will be able to see events in your life or in the world before they happen. Keeping a dream journal and a pen handy will help to develop this skill set. Keep them by your pillow so that they are ready to use when you wake up and need to write in the dark. If a particular dream is important for your conscious mind to remember and interpret, then you will find yourself awake. Immediately upon waking, while the dream is still fresh, write it down, or it will disappear.

You are the Magic

You are the magic wand. You are the one doing all the work. You are the one suffering, clearing, growing, and continuously initiating changes in this lifetime. It is a big calling, and you have to prove yourself ready for every next leap in consciousness.

The process may take a toll on your physical, mental, and emotional health. This is normal during the clearing process of your soul. Remember to take great care of yourself. Drink plenty of water and do what you know you need to do for your health.

When you are called to do greater things, you can expect greater suffering as well. Spirit is generous in understanding, though, and it sometimes gives you little carrots to encourage you as you go. These carrots are signs that higher beings are at work in your life to help.

As you keep working on your clearing, the junk from your soul begins to lessen, your clarity of mind starts to return, and you start to feel 'normal' again in the world. You can see the fruits of your inner metamorphosis and acknowledge them as a blessing. This is your real gift. This is your permanent treasure. No amount of worldly goods can equal this inner treasure.

Dark Night of the Soul is a journey of metamorphosis. This is your Red Pill journey.

How to Heal Yourself

"The Dark Night of the Soul is a purging process that calls us to release all that is unhealed or unnecessary – releasing all that is in the way of our highest good." – Michael Nirdad.

Healing is tricky. It begins when you're down, depressed, and have a lot of emotional processing to do, but it doesn't flourish in this state. You become aware of the need to heal, and you start to question your mind's role in the process. When you're deep in your suffering, the first thing you have to learn is how to grab hold of your mind and reprogram it piece by piece. Until you do, it will run its default programming—which is part of what got you into so much suffering, to begin with.

The good news is that once you see how you have been subconsciously sabotaging yourself and your efforts, you realize that you can turn it around and use the same cognitive machinery in your favor. Everything that feels like it is happening to you, remember, is happening *for* you. It is all happening to open you up to God and your higher self. Don't fight it so hard, for resistance only causes greater pain.

A good spiritual principle here is to remember that what you resist persists. As soon as humanly possible, surrender your soul's journey over to the divine source of energy that pushes all willing beings toward their fullest potential.

Most of us suffer from some form of childhood trauma, either on a micro or macro level. Our parents may have loved us, but not in the way that we needed them to. Or maybe we were bullied in school. Sometimes a seemingly mild event can have psychological repercussions that last and linger for decades. The healing process serves to eradicate these traumas, which have been affecting our mental health covertly under the surface. The healing processes them to light so that we can all live brighter lives. Healing is the final gift. It's the light at the end of the tunnel. When suffering has come and gone, we find ourselves stronger, happier, and healthier than ever before.

The Dark Night of the Soul can feel very negative and even hopeless. It's a period when many of your attachments slip away, leaving you empty and afraid. However, if you focus on the healing that the dark night promises, you can engage with the process with curiosity rather than fear. By focusing on the healing, you keep your attention on the light instead of the dark. This will help to carry you through. But, of course, it's easier said than done. You may be wondering how, exactly, one focuses on healing when it feels like life is slipping through your fingers. It may seem like a fruitless effort, but there are absolutely certain things you can do to lessen anxiety and stay focused on healing.

Let's discuss what we can do to help ourselves. There are to-do's, not-to-do's, and effective and simple healing techniques.

What Not to do:

Don't ignore your issue - Some people are experts at hiding their depression. They would rather bury their emotions than face them. For many of us, this is the more desirable option because facing depression requires work. Depressive emotions are painful. It isn't fun to sit with negativity, but the negativity provides creative options. If you sit with the pain long enough, you'll discover new insights along with newfound motivation. By releasing the emotions, you can cleanse your system and correct your course. But you can't rush this process, and you can't ignore it either. The only way past the darkness is through it. So don't ignore or repress the fact that you're depressed. Acknowledge the pain and get curious about it. You'll discover that you have more strength and power than you ever previously imagined.

Don't drink to excess - Many people turn to drugs and alcohol when they're depressed because substances act as an escape. Through numbing the pain, depressed people attempt to cope through a quick fix. However, quick fixes don't do anything to heal the core issue. Excessive drinking can result in a whole new set of problems. It can tear families apart, destroy the body and the liver, and wreak havoc in several ways. So, avoid creating new problems for yourself through the excessive use of substances. Instead, sit with the pain and find healthy ways to care for yourself.

Don't let your sleeping schedule get out of control. Sleep is so important when you're depressed. Because your mind is suffering, your body needs to be in top form. By yourself, the sleep you need; you're telling yourself that you care about your body. Sleep nurtures your entire system. When you're depressed, however, it's easy to experience restless nights. Your mind may be racing, and you may have trouble relaxing. If this is the case, do whatever you can to make sure your body gets the rest it needs.

Don't lock yourself indoors -It's easy to become a recluse when you feel depressed. Socializing can seem exhausting and far too overstimulating for your sensitive state. However, it is important that you don't lock yourself indoors because socializing is often the thing that has the power to energize you. Humans thrive on connection. They need to be out in the world, interacting with others to feel satisfied. Additionally, exploring the great outdoors is a healthy practice. We feel lighter when we're out in nature. We feel more grounded and more connected to the larger universe around us. So, resist the urge to lock yourself indoors when sadness takes over. Go explore the world. Even if you only have enough energy for a short walk outside, make yourself walk! You'll be thankful you did.

Don't escape too much into video games or other virtual distractions - The world has never been more saturated with distractions. Whether it's our phones, our apps, social media, television, or the news, distractions are all around us at all hours of the day. When we're depressed, it's easy to lean into distractions. Depression eradicates passion. It also depletes us of our energy. So, it makes sense that we would attempt to fill our voids with television and excessive internet use. This is not advised, however, because these distractions are just another quick fix. They don't help the healing process. Escaping into the world of video games could prove healing at first. It may momentarily distract you from your pain. But you can't play video games forever, and if you try to, you will start to feel foggy and lifeless. Use your distractions when you need a distraction. But don't rely on these things like a crutch. The only way past depression is through it. Quick fixes do not address the core issue.

Resist the urge to wallow in sad music - It's important to embrace negative emotions, but it's also important to detach when necessary. Sadness needs to be felt and released, but there's a difference between releasing emotions and wallowing in them. Some people, when depressed, prefer to sit with the sadness and let it consume them. This can lead to feelings of being sorry for oneself. At worst, it results in a sort of pity party. Again, it is productive to sit with emotions, but once you've released everything you can, it's important to get up and move on. Don't get in the habit of wallowing. Let the release act as a source of energy and motivation. Brush yourself off, get back up again, and go experience the world.

Avoid comparing yourself to other people - Comparison is a nasty habit, and yet we're all prone to practicing it. It's easy to look at someone else and think, 'They have it together...why don't I?' Maybe these people appear put together on the outside, with many accomplishments and successes. However, it's impossible to fully understand the experience of another human being. Everyone has their struggles, no matter how polished they may seem on the outside. So, it's often inaccurate to assume someone is in a better position than you are. Comparison is unproductive because, at the end of the day, you're only competing with yourself. So, avoid the habit of comparing yourself to others. Instead, reflect on your own life and the things you want. Then, consider the practical steps you can take to make those wants a new reality.

Don't feel guilty about depression - If you're typically upbeat and social, you may feel guilty about your depressed feelings. You may want to mask your emotions around other people and put on a "happy face." If you tend to be a people-pleaser, this is especially true. But the truth is, everyone experiences bouts of depression, and it's not something to feel guilty about. It's okay to own the fact that you're depressed. Depression is a means toward growth. It serves a purpose in our lives as humans. So don't be ashamed of it. It's an essential rite of passage, and you're a human being just like everyone else. If you have to deny invitations or take moments to yourself at social gatherings, don't be afraid to do so. You must do whatever you can to manage your depression effectively, and that includes owning it and taking responsibility for it.

Don't think too hard about the future - When we're depressed, we tend to overanalyze future possibilities because it gives us hope for a better future. At the same time, though, this can be a defense mechanism because we want to control the future. When we're in stressed or chaotic states, the urge to control life grows even stronger. But unfortunately, we're never able to control our destinies. Therefore, we have no choice but to limit the amount of time we spend hypothesizing about the future. Life happens in the present, and reflecting on the future may feel good at times, but in the end, it's not very productive. Think about what you want your future to look like, and make plans to achieve that. But avoid ruminating on future possibilities. If you spend too much time trying to figure out what's going to happen next, you're only going to make yourself fearful and exhausted. It's a waste of time to put too much weight on things we can't control.

Think carefully about embarking on a new relationship - Relationships are obviously a source of joy and healing, but some relationships also have the power to sabotage our progress. If your depression was catalyzed by the end of a serious or romantic relationship, you should consider pausing before jumping into a new romantic relationship. Sometimes it's hard to know ourselves if we're constantly living for others. Relationships always require sacrifice. And depression usually calls for some selfishness. So, although it's natural to crave new relationships when you're down, you should be honest with yourself and consider the various reasons why you're craving those relationships. What does romance give you that you can't give yourself? What are some other ways you can fill your personal voids? The stronger you are as an independent person, the stronger your relationships will be because you'll be a whole person who knows and understands yourself.

Don't suffer alone - It's easy to withdraw when we're depressed. Our first instinct may be to spend lots of time alone in our rooms. There's still a nasty stigma around depression, which leads people to isolate and shut themselves off from the rest of the world. Some people believe that there is strength in suffering alone, but this is false. When we allow ourselves to be vulnerable, when we share our feelings and allow others to support us, we lessen our own loads and find healing through connection. It may seem scary, but you'd be surprised just how much others are willing and eager to help when you show vulnerability. Humans have a natural desire to help each other. And it's often through sharing in our pain that we achieve the highest level of healing. So, if you incline to suffer alone, try calling a friend instead. Hire a therapist, or phone a family member. These simple acts can do wonders when it comes to accessing strength and inner peace. Through letting others in, we learn that we are not alone in our experiences. Misery loves company, after all.

What to do:

Journaling - You could try journaling during this time to strengthen your connection with yourself. This is how you open up your communication channels. First, you tap into your inner narrative. Write out the contents of your mind. Starting is the hardest part. Once you get going, your subconscious will begin to empty onto the page. Begin anywhere. Begin by writing your dreams or visions. Begin by writing your daily routine. Begin wherever you want as long as you start somewhere.

A journal is also a good place to practice gratitude, which is of the highest vibrational energy in the universe. Be grateful for everything, and write it down. Write down everything you are grateful for, even the small things that seem insignificant. Say, thank you for all of it—the good and the bad, the positive and the negative, the dark and the light.

Write down your prayers, write down your goals, write down the dreams that come to you at night, and spend some time with them. Spend some time with yourself in words, and you will open up your communication quickly. Once you are in connection with yourself, you can begin to open the space between you and your higher self. This will pull in more energy that feeds your budding intuition and self-awareness.

Focus on yourself first - Keep the focus on yourself during this dark time. You're in no shape to take on the suffering or problems of others, for you have plenty of your own to deal with. This is not the time to debate your selfishness versus your selflessness. This is the time for your soul to evolve—and you need all of your energy for this!

Find your Support - Find a new support network. Most likely, you will lose some, if not all, of your usual support, and you will have to look outside of your known social circles for new friends, coaches, and well-wishers. It is of the utmost importance that you do this so that you seek out, find, and accept support in your life. The people who enter your sphere may not be who you expect or even want, but they are there for a reason. The same goes for those who must exit your sphere. Let them go, as it is time for your soul's journey to part from theirs. It does not mean that you will never see them again, although sometimes this is what happens. It just means it's time to part ways with some and walk in stride with others.

If it resonates with you, seek out a spiritual teacher for yourself. A guru or enlightened being with a higher perspective is very helpful if you can find one—or if one finds you.

Music and Dance - There was a period in my life when Music and Dance was my only friend. I forced myself to go out social dancing. I enrolled in social dance classes. Being in the company of other people and in an environment of Music helped me to temporarily forget the trauma in my mind. This helps the mind to recover.

Seek these avenues out. Find ways to incorporate music into your day and life, specifically ways that force you to produce music and rhythm with your body. This is an excellent way to release the stored, blocked emotions that have been dormant in you for years but that are now bubbling up to the surface to be released. Release them. Shake them out of you. The music helps. Plus, you avoid doing further damage to your health.

Engage in social activities - Other people are helpful, too, in a different way. Even though it will present challenges, find social gatherings to attend. If the opportunity arises for you to be social, or at least among others, take it. If you are invited to do something, say yes. Loneliness will only escalate depression and suffering, so take care to alleviate it by being near people when you can. It doesn't have to be a party; any gathering will do. You could even combine it with music and find a class, group, or event that offers music and the company of others. This will divert your attention from the physical, mental, emotional, and spiritual suffering you are in the midst of.

Do what your love - During this time, if something brings you an ounce of joy, take it. Listen to your intuition and your heart, and find the activities that speak to you and that you love. When you find them, keep them, and work them into your routine.

As you suffer, shed, melt, and transform, it is important to take in the joyous feelings, or at least the feelings of calm or neutrality. Allow these energies to fill the space that was once occupied by your former self.

Meditation - The depression that accompanies your soul's suffering can be eased if you take proper care. Psychotherapy, talk therapy, medication, and support groups are good for your mental health. Exercise, yoga, dance, walking, and many other movements also help improve your well-being. Mindfulness and faith practices are all welcome alleviations of depression. Meditation, especially, helps tame the distractions and illusions of the mind. There are many forms of meditation, so find the one that suits you best. Almost anything can be adapted to a meditative practice, even doing the dishes.

The point is that you need to relax. This will allow you to be open and surrender to the process. You need to find a way to release the pressure that has built up from trying to figure everything out and tirelessly thinking yourself into circles. You're burnt out because your mind is on full throttle all of the time, and you need to stop that mental track and begin to watchfully observe your thought patterns and reactions to fully enter the space of transformation. Make relaxation a priority to avoid feelings of hopelessness, dread, and overwhelm.

You may also consider guided meditations. These are great for beginners who want to meditate but feel intimidated or anxious that they may be doing it incorrectly. If that's the case, you can simply find a guided meditation on YouTube, Spotify, or any number of other streaming services. You can also receive a guided meditation from a person in real life. Additionally, you can choose a specific form of guided meditation based on the specific issues you may want to address. There is a wide array of issues that guided meditations cover, including addictions, low self-esteem, anger, anxiety, emotional management, pain management, loss of creativity, and so much more.

Take care of your health - Take conscious action in favor of your health. You don't need to be the hero who slays the beast and fights to obliterate the darkness; that's not what this journey is about. What you need to do is put yourself first and muster all of the strength of heart you can embody.

Be of service - A sure way to feel healing work in your life is to serve others. When you begin to serve the world, the darkness that surrounds you will change. Opening your heart to serve others will not make the darkness disappear—nor should it—but it will bring light into your life.

Be patient - Be patient with yourself. This is one of the greatest virtues.

Healing is a gradual process. Just as you suffer on all levels of being, you also heal on all levels of being. You heal your body along with your mind, emotions, relationships, and spirit. It takes time. The more you know and are aware of what you're going through and why, the better understanding you have of, the bigger processes involved. You are not alone. This is often the first step of finding new meaning to hold onto again after so much suffering. Once that small amount of purpose returns, it gives new hope and positively affects the frustration and sadness you feel, leaving you with a sense of ease. It's like cracking a window for fresh air to circulate into a stale room or opening the door to a dark room just enough for a ray of light to seep in.

Awareness - Close your eyes, and focus on your breath. By focusing on your breath and eliminating all of your outside thoughts, you practice staying in the moment. When you do that enough times, your brain reorients itself. This looks easy, but it takes a lot of practice to quiet the monkey's mind.

It also helps you to observe your thoughts and feelings from a distance. Awareness puts you in a detached state where you're operating from the subconscious rather than conscious reality. For this reason, you can observe your feelings from the outside and learn how to experience them without feeling overwhelmed by them. Overall, awareness does wonders for facilitating a more peaceful and freeing life existence.

Dreams and Visions - Dreams are a window to your soul. I have a book and pen beside my pillow and scribble in my lucid dreaming state. In the morning, I review what I had scribbled in the night and journal them in a proper diary. Have done this for many years. I have developed very good intuition during this process. The more you trust your inner self, the more it gets revealed to you.

Be open to change - It's equally important to stay open in a general sense. As difficult as it may be, try to avoid fighting or resisting the chaos that the Dark Night of the Soul brings. The root of struggle is resistance. So rather than resist, try to embrace the changes that are occurring with curiosity and wonder. Remember that the Dark Night of the Soul is a necessary metamorphosis. Transformation is a natural part of life. If you try to fight the transformation, it will only persist with greater force. So instead, open yourself up and try to float with the changes of the wind. If you lead with the knowledge that life is supporting you and that your soul knows where it needs to go, even if your consciousness is still in the dark, you will have a much easier time embracing the changes that occur. All of the hardships and challenges serve a deeper purpose. Life is leading you toward a road to greater fulfillment. So don't resist the process. The process is your coming home.

When you stop fighting, you allow yourself to be overtaken by the forces at work in your life. Some people talk about surrender as if it means giving yourself over to your enemy, but this is not the case with surrendering to the darkness of suffering in your soul. In this instance, surrender is about ending your resistance, accepting your soul's journey, and letting things happen. When you surrender, you put your trust in the universe and the process.

One of the game-changing perspective shifts we can make on the path of evolutionary awakening is learning to befriend the discomfort that comes with change. If we can start to see this discomfort as something positive and realize that it's a result of the fact that we're growing, it changes everything.

This is, of course, easier said than done. Let's face it: we human beings are animals, and we relate to discomfort as a negative thing. It's part of how we're wired. We're deeply conditioned to believe that feeling bad is bad and feeling good is good. It's one of the most primary orientations to life that all of us have. And this makes sense. Who wants to feel bad? We all want to feel good. It's natural. But it's also natural that a lot of the good things in life—growth, development, and evolution—also come with some degree of feeling bad.

If we want to evolve, we need to shift our perspective so that we can start to see this discomfort more as the natural growing pains that accompany any kind of positive change.

Surrender to the process - Saint Faustina, of the Divine Mercy Devotion, often wrote about the importance of surrendering to suffering. She said, "Oh if only the suffering soul knew how it is loved by God, it would die of joy and excess of happiness! Someday, we will know the value of suffering, but then we will no longer be able to suffer. The present moment is ours."

In response, the Lord says to Saint Faustina, "My daughter, suffering will be a sign to you that I am with you."

Saint Faustina's sentiment implies that the hereafter is the only place where you can awaken to the gifts of suffering, but it also champions the present moment as our time to claim. You can know the value of suffering now, in the present moment. That intelligence is available to you and will help you through the very suffering it entails.

Warrior mindset - You need to develop a warrior's mindset with a single-minded focus. Meditation, hypnosis, support, therapy, and spirituality are all useful weapons to have in your healing arsenal. To specifically target your subconscious mind and reprogram it, you might choose to focus on affirmations or mantras. Repeated sounds or words reconfigure your thought patterns. After resetting your usual thought loops, you can rebuild your mind using a more positive thinking style.

EFT tapping technique - A great complement to these tools is the Emotional Freedom Technique (EFT), often referred to as "tapping." This practice of acupressure uses energy meridians, or pathways in the body, that have been utilized by acupuncturists for thousands of years. By tapping your fingertips on specific areas of the body, you transfer and stimulate energy to course through certain meridians. While you inject this kinetic energy into your physical body, your mental body focuses on the problem you are trying to solve. You might be processing past trauma, a bodily injury, a mental health challenge, or an addiction. Whatever the case, you can use tapping with focused intention and an element of positively charged voice affirmations. This is one of my favorite techniques for quick stress busters. It is also the simplest.

Here's how you do it: choose a finger or multiple fingers, and then choose pressure points on your body. You can choose to tap the skin under your eye or an area on your arm. You can tap your chest or the back of your neck. The important thing is that you're loosening your body and grounding yourself by focusing on real sensations. Some people prefer to tap with just one finger, while others use every finger and multiple pressure points. Additionally, it's suggested that you combine tapping with verbal affirmations. You can tell yourself statements such as, "I am safe" or "let the peace wash over me." You can tailor the affirmations to your specific needs and anxieties. By combining affirmations with physical tapping, you're actually dissolving the emotional blockages and simultaneously stabilizing the mind-body connection. If you benefit from physical actions and practical solutions, tapping may be the perfect thing for you, especially during a Dark Night of the Soul.

Grounding – Usually, during the DNOS process, a person tends to become top-heavy, meaning most of the activity is in the mind or mental activity. When your mind is racing mind, grounding brings you back to the here-and-now and is very helpful in managing overwhelming feelings or anxiety. It is a great way to calm down quickly.

Grounding basically helps to bring your focus to what is happening to you physically, either in your body or in your surroundings, instead of being trapped by the thoughts in your mind that are causing you to feel anxious. It helps you stay in the present moment instead of worrying about things that may happen in the future or events that have already happened.

Sit down in a comfortable chair, one where your feet reach the floor. Close your eyes and focus on your breath. Breathe in slowly for the count of three, then out slowly. Bring your mind's focus to your body.

Take a barefoot walk in the grass, imagining your excess energy is flowing down your feet into the ground. Also, the EFT technique helps; tap with your fingers just below your eyes at the bone. Repeat this for 30sec.

Integrate the process – It is easy to be top-heavy during your DNOS process. I would highly recommend being distracted at least a few times a day so you are not under constant stress. The distractions could include going to a movie, hanging out with people whom you know, go to shopping, walking in the mall or in a park, playing any game you like, engage in some activity like exercise. Force yourself to do some activity at regular intervals. This will keep the mind somewhat distracted, and you will have something to look forward to.

Focus on breathing – One of the most effective and probably the best technique, in my opinion, is paying attention to your breathing. Inhale and exhale consciously. Inhale for a few seconds, hold and then exhale for a few seconds. Doing this just a few times a day will get you back in your physical body. This simple practise will increase your awareness and focus.

Work on suppressed emotions – All of the healing techniques in some way help you release emotions that do not serve you anymore. Here are a few simple practices. Motion releases emotions, dance, jump, run move to get energies moving. Scan your system for stuck energies and visualize the blockages being cleared. Also, you can write down your emotions; this is a form of outlet.

Change your environment - Psychologists believe that our environment has a massive effect on our wellbeing, both on a micro and macro level. For instance, factors such as climate, weather, and social culture play a huge role in facilitating either peace or anxiety in us. This is true on a smaller scale, too, of course. How you decorate your bedroom, the cleanliness of the street you live on, and the amount of clutter in your surroundings also have the capacity to affect your happiness and overall wellbeing. Therefore, if you aren't taking sufficient care of the environment around you, or if you are unhappy with your city or neighborhood, you might consider relocating.

The profound effects of our environments are never more obvious than in the workplace. Most of us spend a great majority of our time at our work locations. And the quality of the work environment can either damage or promote our mental health. If you don't agree with the work culture, for example, you may find yourself feeling excessively irritable. The same goes for dirty or sloppy work atmospheres. Plus, the social energy of a job has the power to enrich or destabilize a person. If you have found yourself in a toxic work environment, don't be afraid to change jobs. No one should have to suffer at the hands of unethical practices or demeaning work cultures. If you would benefit from working from home or in a very specific niche environment, take steps to make that happen. A toxic work environment can destroy one's mental health like no other.

Keep your friends – Your DNOS journey might lead you to be introverted and lonely. This will be difficult for you. I would highly recommend keeping in contact with a few friends who can be there for you when you need them, although they will not understand your process. Your friend(s) can help you to be distracted and engage you in some activity.

Avoid toxic relationships - This is an intricate topic for discussion, and there is no right answer. Relationships are at the core of our spiritual development. It is personal and intimate and varies for each person. Sometimes we find ourselves in an abusive or toxic relationship for a reason. The reason is to learn the lessons that are needed for our Soul growth. It is hard to fathom this when we are in the middle of it. I have been there, and I know this too well.

Depending upon what the Soul has to learn, the toxic relationship may have to be endured. Unfortunately, this has to do with Soul karma, and there is an expiry date for Karma in such cases. This was my experience; I had to be in a relationship that did not make sense to me for a long time. Sometimes you may find yourself at the receiving end of another person's Soul lessons, in which case you do not have to put up with it. You may have to draw your boundaries and lessen/eliminate the impact on your life. If you find yourself in situations where you feel that your energies are depleted in the presence of another person(s), you may want to consider taking action. This could be your work place, your family, your extended family, or your friends. This is your life; you are entirely responsible for all things that happen to you, including your environment and your relationships. I believe in you to take action.

Massage Therapy - Massage therapy works similarly to tapping. Sometimes our bodies need to relax with the help of physical sensation, especially if we're under increased stress or anxiety. Sometimes it's helpful to do more than sit with the feelings and try to analyze them away. If you're an especially physical person, massages may be a helpful means of achieving inner peace and calm. Research suggests that massage has a plethora of healing benefits due to the fact that it releases endorphins, and endorphins are like an organic healer. But it also has a positive impact on mental health, aids in relieving body tension and chronic pain, and helps to alleviate pain brought on by aging. The Mayo Clinic acknowledges massage therapy as a hugely beneficial process. In an article written by the Mayo Clinic press, they state, "Mayo Clinic recognizes the value of massage therapy as an aspect of wellness and has been integrating massage therapy into the hospital setting for almost 20 years."

Hypnotherapy - It's advisable to seek some form of therapy when enduring a period of depression, and the Dark Night of the Soul is no different. Therapy is helpful for a number of reasons. It encourages you to acknowledge your emotions, release them, and receive advice and support from a non-judgmental authority. Hypnotherapy is a specific form of therapy that involves hypnosis as a way to "reprogram" your brain. Dark nights of the soul are especially difficult for those who have childhood traumas.

If you have unresolved traumas from your upbringing, the DNOS may trigger these traumas, and you may benefit from more intensive therapy. If that's the case, hypnotherapy is a great option because it forces you to re-experience the difficult memory and then create new neural pathways associated with it. That way, you can eliminate the possibility of trauma responses.

In a typical hypnotherapy session, the therapist will ask you to describe a past triggering event in vivid detail. Then, they will lead you in a sort of guided meditation. Once you're in that meditative state, by focusing on an object or the therapist's finger, your mind is ready for healing. Your subconscious is closer to the surface than usual, so you have the ability to rewire it. The therapist will typically interject with new thoughts that can form the basis of a new subconscious foundation. For the majority of people, this hypnotherapy process is incredibly healing and effective.

Impact of stress on your physical body - Psychosomatic issues may arise to challenge you. These are physical symptoms that come with no medical explanation and can affect any part of your body. These are psychological issues that manifest as physical symptoms. When you have unresolved emotional issues, psychosomatic symptoms might make themselves known. This is a new way of thinking, and you have to retrain your brain to connect the experience of physical pain with an internal emotional issue that requires your attention.

The science of trauma from studying people with PostTraumatic Stress Disorder (PTSD) reveals that pain experienced in the present time can be caused by traumas that occurred in the past. Many people with chronic pain have a history of mentally suffering from PTSD. Your nervous system is evolved to shift into survival mode when you go through traumatic events. This means that your level of cortisol, a stress hormone, increases and may remain at this sustained, heightened level until well after the event is over. In this condition, your body does not know that the trauma is over, and it has learned to respond in this way. Your blood pressure increases, your immune system weakens, and your healing ability slows. This puts your body in a constant stress state which further feeds your weakening physical health.

It's a cycle, a vicious cycle: compromised health leads to compromised health. The good news is that you can learn to read your body's physical cues as well as your emotional pressure points. The interpretations vary, but you can start to see how things connect in yourself.

Fear manifests as weak kidneys. Worry manifests as a weak heart and brain. Grief infiltrates the lungs. Anger undermines the liver.

Wherever you feel trapped emotions in your body is also where you feel the physical ailments. Your emotional body and your pain body are closely related.

Knee pain is attached to your ego-self. Hip pain means you're afraid to move forward. Hand pain is a sign of imbalance in reaching out to others or receiving help from others. Elbow pain means you are resisting change. If your shoulders hurt, you're carrying too much, and you need to lighten the load.

The physical parts of you are extended metaphors for the mental and emotional parts of you. What you feel in your body can be interpreted literally and figuratively.

If you suffer back pain, it's because you lack emotional support, or sometimes it can mean you lack financial support. You need to feel loved and secure.

Gratitude - Gratitude involves acknowledging the good things that happen, being mindful of present benefits, and recognizing that the sources of goodness are outside us. Many authors and life coaches have described gratitude as a natural feeling that surfaces from within. Most others describe being grateful or ungrateful as a choice. And as a choice, gratitude is an attitude or disposition and is more than an emotional response.

"Gratitude makes sense of our past, brings peace for today, and creates a vision for tomorrow."– Melody Beattle.

Sadhguru explains that gratitude means being receptive to life.

Most people cannot receive something gracefully. Social ethics have taught us that giving is important but taking is not.

Yes, taking is not important; taking is ugly, but receiving is very important; it takes a certain amount of gratefulness and a certain amount of humility.

Just look at any aspect of your life; everything that is worthwhile you are actually receiving. For example, just think about how many people and things were involved in the clothes that you are wearing right now, from the person who planted the cottonseed to the millions of organisms that were involved in making the plant grow, from the people that prepared the cotton, from ginning to weaving to spinning to the clothing maker, agent, distributor, and seller. Even the food that you eat, just for it to get into your system—how many different lives have participated in making this happen?

If you are aware of this and if you receive gracefully, you will be overwhelmed with gratitude. Gratitude is not an attitude; it is something that flows out of you. If it is just a cultivated attitude, it is not of much significance. People have always told you that the magic words are "thank you," but gratitude is not cultivated; it happens when you are overwhelmed by something or somebody.

Suppose you were dying of hunger and somebody gave you a piece of bread; tears of gratitude would come to you. If they had given you that same piece of bread at any other moment, even if they had given you an entire loaf, it wouldn't have meant anything to you. But in that moment of hunger, you would look at the person giving you the piece of bread with enormous gratitude because you are overwhelmed by the experience. Gratitude needs not necessarily find expression in the form of eloquence; it could be just a look, a touch, or a teardrop.

When you have a gratuitous mindset, you focus on the limitless opportunities available in business and life because you already appreciate what you have. When you are grateful, you choose to focus on the positive things rather than the negative things. Gratitude reduces negative thoughts and feelings. Cultivating a mindset of gratitude shifts your focus from yourself to others. Gratitude makes you feel thankful for what you have rather than always wanting more.

Gratitude creates an abundance mindset. When you focus on gratitude, what you appreciate expands and grows.

Gratitude increases your feelings of positivity and appreciation for everything in your life. Choosing gratitude and appreciation can change your life. With gratitude, your first thought is always one of positivity rather than negativity. Engaging in regular gratitude practice can improve your mindset, self-confidence, and perspective. You feel more grateful when you focus on being thankful and feeling positive.

The very process of life is a constant phenomenon of receiving. You have nothing of your own to give; receiving is all you can do. Receive gracefully and share; that's all there is.

Forgiveness - Forgiveness is the flip side of gratitude. It involves responding positively to transgressions by offering mercy instead of vengeance. Like gratitude, it is outward-directed and intentional and recognized as a character strength. Forgiveness is often defined as an individual, voluntary internal process of letting go of feelings and thoughts of resentment, bitterness, anger, and the need for vengeance and retribution toward someone who we believe has wronged us, including ourselves.

Our capacity for forgiveness is a part of human nature that has evolved in the process of natural selection, and according to evolutionary science, it has developed in the same way as our tendency toward revenge. Science says forgiveness brings its array of health benefits, including improved relationships, decreased anxiety and stress, lower blood pressure, a lowered risk of depression, and stronger immune and heart health.

Spiritual teachings have told us that when we hold a grudge and aren't able to forgive, the person it hurts the most is the one holding the grudge.

Forgiveness does not deny pain or wrongdoing; it is a choice to let go of the person who hurt you. - You can feel forgiveness in your body. Think of times in your life when you have forgiven someone and how it made you feel. A part of you that felt heavy becomes lighter.

Forgiveness is not a weakness but rather a sign of great courage and love. Think of how forgiveness can de-escalate negative thinking and situations. Think of this impact on those you are in a relationship with.

Forgiving yourself is one of the hardest things there is to do, but hard is not impossible, we are only human, and sometimes we make mistakes, and sometimes we are weak and do things we know are wrong.

Stop being angry and forgive; you may become that anger; whatever you think about the most will grow. - Acknowledge the issue and the attached pain and anger you feel. You have to be honest with yourself if you truly want to forgive someone. Recognize that healing takes time.

Re-conceptualize the memory. Find a new way to think about the person(s) who hurt you.

Attitude is everything - According to psychologist Robert Puff, our mindset is a huge factor in determining how we cope with major changes and life transitions. He states,

"When big things happen, we tend to think, 'I have a right to be upset.' And it's true—terrible things that happen to us will most likely make us upset—but at the same time, our thoughts create our reality. If we associate experiencing something upsetting with needing to feel unhappy now, perhaps for longer, then this is going to be our reality. No matter the situation, I can almost guarantee you that someone else has gone through the same thing, and they are doing absolutely fine." Puff (2021).

Puff, like most psychologists, believes that it is our attitude, more than anything, which determines our happiness or, alternatively, our unhappiness. So, we are so lucky that we have knowledge about the Dark Night of the Soul. We have examples to study, both in real life and in the fictional stories we consume on a daily basis. We can ease our anxieties through the knowledge that darkness is essential. It leads to progress. With this mindset, we can take control of our dark night in a way that doesn't involve gripping old-life structures. We can find peace by letting go and growing curious.

We always have the ability to reframe our thoughts. So instead of thinking, 'Wow, my is falling apart. What did I do to deserve this?' we can think, 'Wow, life as I knew it is no longer.

What is my soul preparing for me now? What do I want to do with this new freedom?' It's easier to operate from a place of positivity with this new, more optimistic outlook. Curiosity is your best friend when it comes to any major life transition. You might wonder what the caterpillar thinks as it prepares to transition into its cocoon. Is it terrified? Is it worried about the future? Or does it enter its next phase with excitement? Maybe it wonders what colors or patterns will appear on its wings. More than likely, the caterpillar doesn't have the brain capacity to ponder such questions. But even so, it's useful to think about what we gain from worrying. By now, you probably know the answer...there's very little to gain from any form of fear, especially when it comes to the dark times of suffering. We can't predict how our own metamorphosis will transpire, but we can let go and give in to the mystery of the universe. We can choose to trust our souls, which is both the scariest and most exciting thing you can do as a human. If nothing else, choose to give in to the human experience. Otherwise, what's the point of even living?

———— ··•·· ————

We have mentioned a few helpful tools already, but let's really fill in your toolkit.

Awareness is your first tool. Be aware of your feelings and notice when you feel bogged down by the weight of all that you need to let process in your emotions. Until you become aware of your feelings, your mind will run its default program and keep cycling you through the same thoughts and anxieties. Be conscious of your thoughts and change them. Give your attention to the things you want to happen rather than focusing on what you don't want. What you put your attention on is what grows.

Focus on what you do want.

Gratitude and forgiveness are also good tools to use often. Get in the habit of being grateful for what you have, and forgive the people and things in your life that could otherwise nag and distract you. Forgiveness is a gift you give yourself, for often, the person you direct it to does not deserve such grace. Forgive so that you may clear your mind and heart from negativity.

Your support system is another tool for healing, including friends, family, teachers, a guru, and yourself. You are your biggest support. Take care of how you communicate with yourself internally. Pay attention to your dreams, visions, and intuitions. This is how you build a trusting relationship with yourself. Then, by extension, you will know how to strengthen your relationships with others. Be social; it helps heal the loneliness that comes with suffering. Force yourself to be social if you have to. Schedule social events. They will occupy your mind and fill some of the negative space with positive experiences.

Prayer and asking for guidance are tools. They alert your higher power that you need help—but remember that you do need to ask in order to receive.

Self-care is a tool for healing.

Try hypnotherapy, a professionally guided hypnosis that will put you into a state of deep relaxation where you can process the big emotions that need to be released.

Try meditation. If you try one style and don't like it, try another one. Try breathing meditations, moving meditations, and relaxing meditations. Try everything. Guided meditations are abundant online and on various apps. Consult your doctor as needed. God helps those who help themselves, do not avoid Doctors or medication when needed.

Try a massage. The benefits are numerous. Massage reduces anxiety and depression. It eases insomnia, soothes muscles, and provides relief from arthritis and other ailments. The tactile nature of massage is healing. Human touch is healing, especially touch that presses the nerve endings in your skin to stimulate the release of your "feel good" endorphins. Massage can improve how you breathe, metabolize, and circulate blood and nutrients. It stimulates your body's natural cleansing systems while improving your movement and flexibility.

In the spirit of self-care, sometimes you need to add a change of environment to your toolkit. Change is good, especially if it removes you from a toxic situation, perhaps one you were not even aware of until you have some space from it.

Your complete health and well-being come from all parts of you. Keep your body healthy with movement, nutrition, and rest. Keep your mind healthy with conscious mindfulness practices and positivity. Keep your emotions healthy by caring for yourself and allowing your emotions to release and process. Keep your relationships healthy with attention to boundaries, communication, and interactions that serve who you are becoming. Keep your spirit healthy by listening to and nurturing your soul's desires.

CONCLUSION

"Have Faith: Bright morning comes right after a dark night."- Trinity Royal.

The Dark Night of the Soul is an essential rite of passage. I've stated it already, but it bears repeating. Everyone must endure it at one point or another. Everyone must transform t grow, and ascend. Each of us is part of a massive and complicated web. We're all connected as part of one larger organism. Our souls reveal a story that is simultaneously personal and universal. We must work with our free will to make our lives what we want them to be, and we must also surrender to fate when necessary. It's all a delicate balance, and it's natural to miss some steps along the way. However, the Dark Night of the Soul is a profound human experience. If you are in the midst of your own dark night, understand that you are in the process of turning a corner. You're on your way to discovering new purpose and meaning. In essence, you're on the evolutionary fast track.

Life occurs in cycles. And if you take the time to reflect on past experiences, you'll notice this with startling potency. More likely than not, you've already overcome various life hurdles that share a stark resemblance to a Dark Night of the Soul. Perhaps your parents got divorced when you were a child, or you switched schools and suffered through a terrible readjustment period. Maybe you went through a horrible breakup or left all of your friends to go to college in a new city. These experiences can provide insight and strength when you're worried about particularly challenging transitions. Hopefully, you survived these similar experiences from your past and even learned important lessons from them. You can apply that same awareness to your own Dark Night of the Soul and use it as motivation to get curious. What have the themes of your life been up until this point? Have your previous transitions taught you something about how you navigate relationships? Or about how you navigate success? Or maybe they've revealed something about your own personal psychology. Think back to your past and search for wisdom. You'll be surprised at how much solace this practice can bring when life feels chaotic and unmanageable.

Your Dark Night of the Soul is your saving grace. It's your ticket to a richer, more meaningful experience as a human being here on earth. You have the chance to discover what truly makes your heart sing. Furthermore, you have the opportunity to develop lifelong strength, the strength that will carry you through any more deeply future obstacles with wisdom and clarity. You deserve to live life in a deeper way. You deserve to live beneath the surface of mundane reality. Instead of feeling sleepy, you should be energized. Instead of feeling complacent, you should be passionate. The darkness grants us the opportunity to become truly alive. And there's nothing greater in the world than feeling truly alive. It is our God-given right and our soul's fuel for growth. We're here on earth to grow. So, give in to the natural process, accept the highs and lows, and embrace the life that burns like fireworks beneath our skin. That is the purpose of the soul's journey, and we're all lucky to be a part of it.

Why would your soul's journey lead you to suffer?

This book has given you the answer—it is to heal you.

Healing is a process. The Dark Nights of the Soul and healing begin at some point and end at another, weaving in and out of each other as they go.

- You are in the cocoon, almost a butterfly, strengthening the wings that will fly you.

- The home you knew and found comfort in is gone, destroyed, and you are lost, searching for a new home that is built on the solid, true ground.

- You are scraping off dead layers of your old self so you can more fully embody your new, higher self.

- You are a diamond who outlasts great time and pressure.

As the Diamond in you begins to shine, you know that this arduous suffering journey was worth it. The fruits of your labor are far more than your physical senses understand. You have built a foundation that stands Eternal in the core of your being. You are a Diamond shining brightly, radiating light merely by your presence. You are Home. You have been through a Metamorphosis process. You are the One you have been waiting for.

THANK YOU

I want to personally Thank you for reading this book.

I have poured my Heart and Soul into these pages. I hope you have gained some valuable insights from the information presented. Please consider leaving your valuable review. Your review and feedback are important to me. Thank you so much.

⭐ ⭐ ⭐ ⭐ ⭐

Scan to leave a review:

Preview Chapter from Book - From Suffering to Healing

Chapter 7: Finding the Gifts in Darkness

*We rarely find people who achieve great things
without first going astray.* — Meister Eckhart

You come to the darkness to resolve your personal set of
circumstances. No matter what desires drove you there or
what obstacles slowed you down, you encounter suffering
for the purpose of balancing your soul's karmic existence.
This is the gift of suffering. You gain freedom through the
darkness.

There is a distinct possibility that you emerge from darkness into a transformed state of consciousness. On the other side of suffering, life has meaning again. It's no longer a conceptual meaning, though; it's not something you can necessarily explain, either. Its meaning is much deeper than you can readily access with your mind, and it brings a profound sense of purpose and connectedness with a life that is greater than you've ever experienced. Your life is no longer dependent upon the things you thought were important. Your rebirthed self is different.

Your soul's suffering is a kind of death. Parts of you have died. The previous version of you is dead. The egoic sense of self is extinguished, and your truest self has emerged.

Like many other people who endure this transformation, you come through the darkness and realize that you had to suffer to experience your spiritual awakening. The suffering was part of your awakening; it was part of your strengthening. It was a time of great struggle where you amassed a wealth of knowledge and self-discovery.

The darkness that your soul journeys through contains many gifts. This stage of personal development causes you to undergo a significant transition to a deeper understanding of your life and your place in it. These are valuable gifts on your soul's journey. The struggle you confronted when you faced your shadow and all of the repressed parts of yourself had meaning. The fears, desires, traumas, and beliefs that broke through from inside of you and rippled out into your reality to be resolved all have meaning. They all come with a great reward—for as painful as your suffering has been, the fruition is unbelievably empowering and liberating.

A time of dark suffering in your soul is not a problem that you have to solve. Sometimes, you will get a peek at the darkness within you and think that you have to eradicate it. Maybe you tell someone or bring it up in therapy, and you reason through it until you can put it out of your mind and feel relief that it is over. It isn't over, and it hasn't even begun. Your ego-self wants to control your relationship with darkness, but it has no power over your soul or your soul's journey. If you are given a glimpse into your shadow, take it for what it is and allow it to exist. Sit with it, don't run away from it.

The weight of what your shadow holds is oppressive and holding you down, and relief from the pressure is not always easy to come by. You might begin by looking for help outside of yourself because this is what you have been trained to do in your human existence thus far.

Remember, your suffering is not for God, nor does it serve God. The suffering is for you and will serve you and everyone you interact with, by extension. Everyone who experiences a deep struggle in their soul creates their answer to the question of why it happens. No one's answer is right, and no one's answer is wrong. All solutions are the ego's and mind's attempt to create meaning out of chaos, which is what they're good at doing.

Your suffering is the epitome of a blessing in disguise. Wrapped in darkness and depression, it removes the ground from beneath your feet and leaves you to experience suffering in your soul. It leaves you there, illuminating the parts of you that are fearful, fragile, decaying, and in desperate need of change and growth. When it tries to claim these things from you, it only leaves you feeling more empty inside. Then, from somewhere deep in that dark void, from nowhere that ever existed before, from the mere potential of a shred of hope, a new seed is planted in you. This seed contains the true peace and joy that come from being aligned with your soul's purpose, and then you know you are blessed.

People can endure unimaginable ordeals and still manage to discover their talents and contribute to humanity's progress in a striking way. History provides many examples of exemplary individuals who suffered greatly—or who suffered in any capacity at all—and still went on to use their gifts to achieve greatness.

Abraham Lincoln is one outstanding example. His early life was surrounded by death and loneliness, and his adult life was weighed down by war and the death of thousands of young soldiers. He was known to be a melancholic man who suffered through the darkness, and still, he became an icon of wisdom and leadership. One theory says that the efforts he made for his country were what helped him escape his melancholy. Another idea is that the darkness itself was the ground upon which he grew his leadership. Either way, he once said, "If there's a worse place than hell, I'm in it."

Nelson Mandela is another strong example of someone whose suffering did not deter his significance. He was imprisoned for 27 years under harsh conditions, yet he never lost his vision or sense of destiny. A younger prisoner who knew Mandela said of him, "...he has a tremendous presence, apart from his bearing, his deportment, and so on. He's a person who's got real control over his behavior. He is also quite conscious of the kind of seriousness he radiates."

Maya Angelou is another intriguing example of how a dark time of suffering in the soul leads to a transformative presence in the world. As a child, she did not speak for a period of a few years. Her guilt and wounds of abuse kept her silent. As an adult, she recited the inaugural poem for President Bill Clinton, and her words inspired millions to make something of their soul's suffering. In all of her public appearances, she showed both the pain and the joy that shaped her mission in life. She carried her pain with her throughout her life, yet her joy seemed to increase with her impact on people from around the world. In her suffering and metamorphosis, she had her voice taken away from her and then returned with added strength and magnitude.

J.K. Rowling is another shining example. When she was trying to pitch *Harry Potter and the Philosopher's Stone*, she was on government assistance with young children. She was broke. She couldn't afford to make copies of her book to send out to publishers. Instead, she manually re-typed every single copy of the lengthy novel. She was rejected dozens of times, but she never gave up, and you know how that story ends: Rowling went on to become the first self-made billionaire author.

Jim Carey has led a transformational life, too. When he was 14 years old, his father lost his job, and his family became impoverished. Carey moved to Los Angeles when he was 16 years old to take a chance at his acting dreams. He wrote himself a fake check for $10 million to inspire himself to never give up, and he kept it with him in his wallet. It took him another 16 years before starring in his first hit movie, *Dumb and Dumber*. His father was the one who encouraged him to follow his dream, and when he died, Carey buried the fake check with him in his casket.

Oprah Winfrey is a great example of perseverance as well. Growing up, she was a victim of sexual abuse. Despite her incredibly challenging upbringing, she was an honors student in high school and earned a full scholarship to college. She didn't stop there: She climbed her way up the television network world and is one of the wealthiest people in the world and one of the most influential icons.

Michael Jordan is arguably the greatest basketball player of all time. He was once cut from his high school basketball team, but he never quit; he just worked harder. His desire was stronger than anything else. Jordan went on to become an NCAA star, a six-time NBA champion, and an MVP in multiple leagues, and he was inducted into the Basketball Hall of Fame.

John F. Kennedy also endured sustained suffering before becoming a cultural icon. In his youth, before anyone knew of him as the President of the United States, Kennedy suffered a plethora of physical illnesses, including chronic back pain. His health was poor, so he had to sneak his way into the US Navy to fight during World War II. He survived this and more on his soul's journey.

Mother Teresa of Calcutta is another example of someone who endured the darkness of deep suffering in her soul for decades. According to her letters, life was a struggle for her. She could not easily embrace the soul's journey, and this was during a time when there was much less discussion circulating about such spiritual matters. The darkness in her soul captured her after she found her "call within a call" and began her mission to serve the poorest of the poor in Calcutta, India. After hearing the call and receiving its message, she was still unable to feel the presence of God in her life. Through her suffering, she continued to follow God's will but also questioned the very existence of that God. In one of her letters, published in her book, *Come Be My Light*, Mother Teresa wrote, "In my soul, I feel just that terrible pain of loss—of God not wanting me—of God not being God—of God not really existing." Her journey of persevering faith is considered one of the longest recorded instances of a Dark Night of the Soul.

Eckhart Tolle is an exemplary model of a contemporary spiritual healer and leader. He turned the experience of his inner turmoil into a career as an author and teacher who has reached millions of people with his transformative work.

He thinks of deep suffering as a breakdown of the meaning of life. It explodes into your life, covering everything with meaninglessness. An external event triggers it, and everything in your life that was meaningful collapses inexplicably. He also says it feels like depression. The true disaster is the collapse of the conceptual frameworks that held your life together formerly. These are the meanings that your mind ascribes to different facets of your life. They all cave in, and you're left in the dark with the rubble. But you go into the suffering with the definite possibility that you will also come out of it, and life takes on a different sort of meaning that is not easily communicated in the usual language of conceptual thinking. You are re-birthed with greater connectedness, detached from your egoic sense of self. It is a death, and death is painful.

Of course, you can collapse old conceptual meanings in other ways that don't include great suffering. The very first lesson in *A Course in Miracles*, a popular spiritual self-help program, is to intentionally collapse the meanings of life that your mind made up. You practice by looking at different objects in the room and saying, "This doesn't mean anything; that doesn't mean anything." This is a small, benign rehearsal compared to the forced collapse of deep suffering, but it does help you understand the working and reworking of your mind.

Additionally, there is a story in the bible, in the book of Corinthians, where Paul is afflicted by a thorn in his flesh. At the peak of his highest height, he is stabbed by an incurable thorn. He pleaded with God to remove it. According to the Bible, he did this at least three times, but God couldn't remove it. Removing it would eradicate the lesson that Paul was meant to learn, the lesson of grace. According to the passage, God stated, "My grace is sufficient for you, for my power is made perfect in weakness." Later, in Romans, Paul utters the sentiment that neither "height nor depth" can "separate us from the love of God in Christ." So, you see how there's a symbolic suggestion here. Paul's story illuminates something about the soul's journey and purpose. His story suggests something about the way our human suffering not only humbles us but also fuels us. The statement about power being made perfect in weakness is especially profound, given our understanding of the soul's journey.

We need our weaknesses in order to discover our strengths. When we are in the midst of a Dark Night of the Soul, we become very aware of our weaknesses. It is typically a period when our self-esteem and confidence are at an all-time low. But the goal is not to do away with our weaknesses completely, but rather to look for God's grace in the midst of it. Sometimes it is the reflection on our weaknesses which motivates a new career or life direction. You may decide to become a wounded healer, for example. In that way, you alchemize the wound into a gift that can guide others. We can't plead our wounds and weaknesses away, but we can allow them to make us whole. We can grant them the ability to give us strength, and we can use that strength to make a difference in the world. That is the lesson of Paul's thorn.

Finally, a similar theme comes to the surface when you explore the story of Christ. On the one hand, the story of Jesus is tragic. Bursting with compassion and understanding, Jesus made it his sole mission to spread love and lead by example. He healed through love and inspired a nation by preaching his God-given wisdom. But in the end, he was crucified for his pursuits. He was forced to suffer and even die by the very people he was trying to save. But following his death, he was resurrected, which reveals something about the human soul. Sometimes a part of us needs to die in order to mold and live out our mission with renewed power. Without Christ's resurrection, there would be no glory. This reveals something about our personal crosses that we all must bear. If your ego-self does not die, there is no space for a metamorphosis. And without metamorphosis, there is no growth. No evolution. Ortlund (2021).

It can be difficult to stay in tune with our divine natures when everything is going right or according to plan. It's easy to take things for granted or lose sight of the truth at these junctures. But when the chips are low, our egos are ripe for molding. It's easier to surrender to a higher purpose because all of our previous attachments are lost or given new meaning. This can provide comfort if you are in the middle of your own Dark Night of the Soul. Suffering serves a purpose, and it acts as the necessary precursor to life's bounty and gold. Jesus knew this. Paul knew this. And many others learned through the process of their own dark nights. So long as you can find grace amidst the struggle, you'll emerge anew. You'll have more strength and more certainty than ever before.

The list is infinite. The amount of people who have suffered greatly and gone on to do even greater things in life and for others is endless.

What is your gift in the darkness?

Preview from Book - Lucifer Rebellion. Christ vs Satan-Final Battle for Earth has Begun

Chapter 10 - Clarion Call from GOD to all the Angels in Heaven

> "What takes place on Earth is very important to Heaven." - Trinity Royal

In the previous chapters, you've learned about the spiritual forces at play throughout history and in the world right now. Even though they are unknown to the vast majority of humanity, you have chosen to open your eyes and discover how they have been and are influencing you and everyone around you. As Morpheus would say, You have taken the red pill.

With the knowledge you now possess, it is time to move on to more advanced topics where you will gain significantly more depth of knowledge. While you've learned about the spiritual Matrix, and how Dark-aligned and Light-aligned entities influence Earth-whether by enslaving humans or liberating them, encouraging selfishness rather than altruism, and so on, now you'll see specific instances of these activities–and the rationales behind specific plans launched by both sides in the war– especially centering around Jesus Christ and His teachings.

Why God Needs Your Help

We have seen in the previous chapters that the War came to be centered on planet Earth. Earth is the epicenter of the battle between Dark and Light. What happens here affects the rest of the Universe.

Due to this, the human race has become God's prized possession, and our planet Earth– also called Urantia in higher realms of consciousness–is the site of many of God's most important plans and a storehouse of His most valuable resources. For the purposes of this book, we don't need to go too far into the details of the Universal Father's creative activity, or every one of His agents. Here, we will simply go over the broadest, most basic points of Earth's history you need to know to get a grasp of what you need to do to help the forces of Light.

God's own son "the Son of God" is Christ, who is also the creator of the Universe. Millions of years ago, Christ manipulated many nebulae to form stars, and thus our galaxy, and around one of these stars at the edge of one of these galaxies is the Milky Way. Each galaxy consists of numerous solar systems and planets.

When our Creator created this planet, He noted that there was something special about this little blue orb, it became known as the "seed" planet. The seed planets are considered special as new souls are developed on these kinds of planets. The seed planets are the training ground for young Souls on an evolutionary path. There are very few in number in this part of our galaxy. Christ with the help of Trinity consciousness (God the Universal Father, Eternal, Son, and Infinite Spirit) created the Human species. So we are created in His "likeness" as the scriptures state, making the residents of our planet particularly important for the plans of both God and Satan.

Human beings evolved empathy, compassion, altruism, and especially religious feelings much earlier in our development than was the case for sentient beings in other worlds. As a result, the spiritual energies produced by the development of human souls, whether ascending towards higher consciousness realms as the Light desires or chained down to this lower dimensional consciousness as the Dark desires, far outweigh those produced by even heavenly beings in the universe. Since the war has been at a stalemate in the rest of the Universe for a very long time, with neither Lucifer's forces nor the Light has been able to dislodge the other, Earth has taken center stage as the decisive point. Darkness, unfortunately, has managed to make significant in-roads on our planet and has advanced its plans very far. On the other hand, the Universal Father has plans of his own involving His most powerful agent here: Jesus Christ, whom we shall learn more about in future chapters. This should suffice as an overview of the Universal Father treasures humanity in particular so much.

Effects of the Rebellion

Now, due to Lucifer's rebellion, discussed in previous chapters, God has had a very difficult time reaching out to humanity, protecting and guiding us, despite how highly He valued us. The path for growth toward the Light was growing harder and harder for us, with many obstacles placed in our way. Here are some of the ways Darkness has interfered with us:

- No real religious teachings. There have been many great religions started by enlightened prophets which have been stamped out by the Dark. Humanity has been made to forget these religions and their teachings to delay the growth of many strong souls and prevent knowledge about the great spiritual conflict from spreading widely.

- Manipulation of teachings. Cunning agents of Darkness have manipulated some teachings of religions throughout history–and in the present day–to sow confusion and make it even harder for seekers to attain genuine knowledge of Heaven and higher spiritual realms.

- Over-emphasis on the process: Partially due to machinations from the Dark, but also due to honest mistakes which built up over time, much of humanity has become too focused on ritual–rather than finding their own individual "spark" of God within themselves.

Finally, whereas direct communication with God is possible on higher realms that are more vibrationally attuned to Paradise–the Veil or Matrix which envelopes Earth has cut us off from the Divine in some way. Only if we are very fortunate can some of us access higher realities, and often only in dreams; communion with the Universal Father Himself is very rare, with only the Bestowal of Christ giving us hope (described in the next chapter).

Even so, there are some agents of the Light who have come to Earth to assist us in reaching higher consciousness levels, even if they were not in direct contact with the Divine. Some gods in ancient polytheistic or henotheistic religions were heavenly messengers who came to help Humanity in the evolution process. Also religious figures like Lord Buddha or Lord Krishna, philosophers like Aristotle, Plato, Zeno of Elea, Confucius, and some modern-day personages like Martin Luther King. Some angels even gave inspiration to great inventors and teachers, like Jonas Salk–creator of the polio vaccine, Albert Einstein, and other Nobel Prize winners.

All these people were sent or influenced by the Light to guide mankind towards the climactic event which will occur soon, in the present time we are living in. The Dark has also influenced our world in many ways, both enslaving individual humans, trapping their souls, encouraging the evolution of dark cults, and, teaching other individuals selfish methods of increasing their power and influence. Some Dark agents manifested in this world directly, putting on human disguises, while others merely contacted ordinary people seeking power and subtly guided them into the shadows. Many Dark agents or servants settled as kings, queens, or great and bloody conquerors. Adolf Hitler and Ghenghis Khan are two such examples. Less famously, Dark agents generally tried–and are still trying–to infiltrate large, powerful, centralized governments to control information and how people lived, to ensure as few as possible could ascend. They also manipulate the genetic code of humanity, to cut out strands of DNA carrying Light codes–such as nobler, more altruistic temperaments, higher attunement to spiritual realities, a higher propensity to dream–and so on.

Despite both sides doing their best throughout hundreds of thousands of years, Light was never able to break Dark's grasp on the world, and Dark could never remove every trace of Light from Earth, even as its influence steadily grew. Thus, the war on Earth was grinding down into a stalemate as well; whatever advantages Dark had would take many, many centuries to come to fruition. Before that can happen, the forces of Light desire to strike a shattering blow against Satan/Lucifer. The fallen Morning Star, cunning as he is, anticipated that, and is attempting to gather his forces for his decisive annihilation of Light on Earth, which will allow him to capture the planet and turn all of the prodigious energy humans produce into his ends.

God's Counterattack

As the situation on Earth is rapidly heating up, the Universal Father focused more and more of His energies and attention on it. About 200,000 years ago, He made a clarion call to all of His angels to focus on humanity and do all they can to uplift the consciousness of this blue orb. God is no fool and made clear to His angelic forces that this would likely be the most difficult mission they had ever attempted ever in their entire existence. God also emphasized to them this struggle was worth it, for He realized how unique and powerful humanity is due to its peculiar evolutionary history, and thus He loves humanity and Earth more than any other place in the Universe. Much of God's focus is on humanity and earth at the present time. This is an absolute fact.

This clarion call rang out wide to all of Heavens and Paradise. The mission was simply to save Humans and Earth. A mission like this was never attempted in the history of creation.

Since this was unique, a vast number of angels had no idea what to expect and did not sign up for the mission. Given the incredible skills, the angels possessed, very many of them could not take it for fear of the unknown. Many were afraid of the struggle and Satan's forces in general and were also uncertain of the outcome. Most have already witnessed the devastation caused by Lucifer's rebellion in the Heavens. After all, such an endeavor had never been attempted before, and no histories existed in the great archives and annals of Heaven that could give any guidance on a war like this. The angels who raised these concerns did not have full faith in the Universal Father's victory, so they chose to sit out the battle and wait and see who would win. Others did not want to limit their consciousness by focusing on one planet in one system in one planet of the vast Universe.

In fairness to these seemingly cowardly angels, fighting Satan's forces on Earth is a truly monumental task. The Matrix surrounding Earth has several characteristics that make things harder for the Light than the Dark.

However, some angels did have faith in God and Christ and said "yes" to this divine mission. There were at least 144,000 of these according to the Holy Bible. These are the angles who have agreed to come into the Matrix and be part of the Matrix, mingle with evolving Human souls, and increase the vibrations of Human consciousness thereby helping God and the cause of light. These angels were known as descended angels. According to a divinely orchestrated plan, these brave angelic souls planted themselves at predetermined strategic points of Human evolution to become teachers, preachers, inventors, gurus, sadhus, scientists..etc. Basically to teach and help evolve Humanity.

> Then I looked, and behold, the Lamb was standing on Mount Zion, and with Him one hundred and forty-four thousand, having His name and the name of His Father written on their foreheads. – Revelations 14:1

However life is not all rosy for these brave angels; by being in the Matrix, all of them got caught up in the illusion of the Matrix, and most if not all forgot their divine origins and inter-mingled with humans over the period of 200,000 years. This has helped to manipulate the DNA of the Human species, thereby evolving the human species faster and closer to God. If Light wins, these brave angels will enjoy all the splendor and accolades they have earned.

The Matrix prevents spiritual beings from heavenly realms from passing into Earth. They are only allowed in if a resident of Earth, within the Matrix itself, specifically asks them to enter. This is called the doctrine of non-interference. Some beings can get around this, but it is extremely rare, and Dark forces like demons and shadow-whisperers more often do this. The great Bestowal of Christ was one exception to this rule in Light's favor. Another exception was the case of 'original seeders,' angels who visited humanity in distant past eons to place Light information in our genomes.

The effects of the Matrix on the development of the soul itself present another obstacle to the cause of Light due to loss of memory. Souls, ignorant as they are, cannot easily coordinate with each other, or angelic beings, and must rely on their internal abilities to evolve, which can be made easier if the bodies to which they are reincarnated possess useful strands of Light-aligned DNA. In this regard, humans possessing these types of DNA should mingle as much as possible with the rest of the human population to spread them far and wide and to future generations, but again, since accumulated knowledge is lost, this is harder to do. Souls must also learn their own lessons, rather than being taught, how to avoid the pitfalls of the Dark, transform Dark energies into Light ones, and enhance the collective consciousness of humanity.

Given all this, you can imagine why God is personally concerned with this war on a single small planet and refuses to give up on the human race. It is extremely important for Him and the Light to win this war, as so many of His strongest angels have already invested so much. In other words, not only are human souls at stake, but Paradise and other types of angels from higher heavenly realms also have vulnerable souls that might be at risk if they lose. Thus, God has a vested interest in you—yes, you! He wants your soul to grow, advance, and improve your spiritual life so you can help in the struggle. This will determine whether Light or Dark wins in the end.

If you like this preview...you will love this book. Get it today

From Suffering to Healing

Scan Me

"I highly recommend this for anyone *who has ever suffered in their lives*, and, in all honesty, who hasn't?"

Why do **bad things happen to good people**?

Why does your **Life journey lead you to suffer?**

The Answer is to Heal You.

Your suffering is the epitome of a **blessing in disguise.** Wrapped in darkness and suffering, it removes the ground from beneath your feet and leaves you fearful, fragile, and devoid of meaning in life.

Most beings that we adore or worship have gone through dark times in their life. This includes Christ, Buddha, Gandhi, Nelson Mandela, Oprah, Abraham Lincoln, etc. This process is necessary as it redefines a person, re-makes one character, and chips away the darkness to bring out the luster of your **Real Self.** This is your **METAMORPHOSIS**.

Welcome to Heaven. Your Graduation from Kindergarten Earth to Heaven

Scan Me

"I go and prepare a place for you, I will come back and take you to be with me that you also may be where I am." - John 14:3

Ever wonder **if Heaven is real**? What **proof** do we have?

How does one **go to Heaven**? What are the **minimum requirements for Heaven**?

Why <u>**Life of Earth is your Kindergarten school**</u>?

Trinity explores the following:

- Isn't Heaven **just a mind concept**? *What is the proof of its existence? Why do I even bother about Heaven? What is in it for me?*

- What are the **minimum requirements to go to Heaven or the ticket booth to Heaven?**

- Why is life on Earth your **kindergarten school?**

- Are there **different levels to heaven? If so, how many? What are they?** Does the **time and space continuum exist in Heaven?** *If so how different is it compared to Earth's time and space?*

Your Life in Heaven. Family, Marriage, Sex, Work

"No eye has seen, no ear has heard, and no mind has imagined what God has prepared for those who love him." – 1 Corinthians 2:9

Ever wonder what your **life in Heaven will look like after your mortal death**?

Is there **Marriage** in Heaven? Do you have a **Family in Heaven**?

Do you have your **Parents or kids or your siblings** in Heaven?

Do you have **Sexual intercourse** in Heaven?

And what do you do all day? Is there a **daily Job**? Oh. And will you meet your **deceased family members**, friends, and relatives?

These are questions that curious minds like me ask. You will find **authoritative un-speculated** answers here.

SOS - Save yOur Soul

"For what shall it profit a man, if he shall gain the whole world, and lose his own soul?" - *Mark 8:36*

Ever Wonder **What Happens After You Die**? Is it the end?

What did **Christ** Say about death and life after mortal death?

Is there a way to Save yOur Soul? If so How?

What exactly is **Soul** and **Spirit**, is it just a new age concept? What did Christ Say?

Trinity considered to be one of the bridges between Heaven and Earth, shares general Angelic knowledge. This book explores:

What are the unseen parts of us that make us who we are? What is left behind after Mortal death and what happens to these **unseen parts of us**?

What exactly is **Soul** and **Spirit**, is it just a new age concept? What did Christ Say? Is there a way to Save yOur Soul? If so How? Does Heaven actually exist? Can a ticket to Heaven be guaranteed?

Lucifer Rebellion. Christ vs. Satan – Final Battle for Earth Has Begun

Multiple Award-winning Book

"extraordinary book"   "Definitely a five-star read"   - [International Review of Books]

Ever wonder **why there is a War between GOD and the Devil?** Ever wonder how the **War in Heaven started or what the Lucifer Rebellion is**?

Ever wonder why War in heaven came to Earth or why darkness still exists on Earth? And why did God send Christ to Earth?

This book explores:

- How and Why did the **war in Heaven start**? How did the War in Heaven come to Earth?

- Why did **God send Christ** to planet Earth? Was it to save Humanity and the Universe?

- What exactly happened during **Christ's First Coming** event? What is expected during the Second Coming event?

Trinity takes us on a **journey beyond time and space** to find the answers to these questions that every believer should know.

Lucifer Rebellion. Christ vs Satan – The Second Coming of Christ

Scan Me

Ever wonder **why there is a War between GOD and Devil?**

Ever wonder how the **War in Heaven started or what Lucifer Rebellion is?** **and why War in Heaven came to Earth** and why darkness still exists on Earth?

This book explores:

- How and Why did the **war in Heaven start**?

- How did the War in Heaven come to Earth?

- Why did **God send Christ** to planet Earth? Was it to save Humanity and the Universe?

- What are the effects of War on Earth and in Heaven?

- What exactly happened during **Christ's First Coming** event?

- What is expected during the Second Coming event?

I invite you to join me on a journey beyond space and time when the Lucifer Rebellion started and the reasons for Christ's First and Second Coming events.

Christ & Demons - Unseen Realms of Darkness

"The reason the Son of God appeared was to destroy the Devil's work." -Ephesians 6:12

Is there an **UNSEEN world of Darkness** hidden in front of our eyes?

Ever wonder why **Evil** exists on Earth? Ever wonder how **Satan got to planet Earth** and what exactly is the Dark Empire Agenda?

Ever wonder why Christ chose planet Earth for His great Bestowal?

What is the **agenda of Darkness**? Why do God and Christ let dark forces flourish on Earth? Does God have a plan? What is it?

What are the differences between **Demons, Evil Spirits, and Ghosts**? How does **Selling one's Soul to the devil** happen?

Son of Man becomes Son of God. One Event that Changed the History of the World

<u>Award-Winning Book</u>

"an opportunity for the reader to embark on a journey with Him, feel what He feels"

"A fascinating description and story of how Christ emerged, changed and developed into the highest of holiest beings, second only to God."

"An exceptional and well-written novel without the preaching and pointless prose and verbiage of others of this type"

There is **ONE event** that is the true turning point in the history of Earth. This is not the Birth or Baptism of Jesus, but it is the **fight with the Devil**

Ever wonder what would have happened to Earth if Christ failed against Satan? This was a real possibility, although it is considered blasphemous to talk about it.

What Happened on Easter Saturday? 36 hr mystery between Death and Resurrection

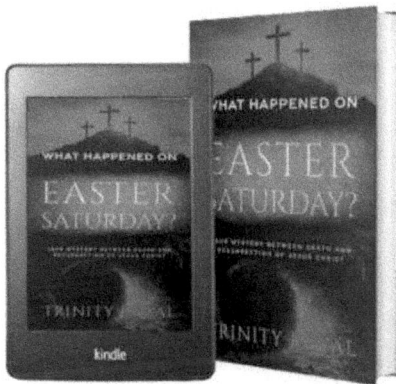

Scan Me

"*A five-star read, absolutely.*"

"**It stands to reason that Saturday was a critical time for Him**"

"I highly recommend this incredible book as it takes the reader through both the physical and spiritual journey of Him as he underwent His transformation. **A five-star read, absolutely.**"

"I for one never really thought about that Saturday, so for me **it was a riveting experience**, learning about that previously overlooked time."

Ever wonder **what happened when Christ was inside the Tomb for 36 hrs** between death and resurrection?

Ever wonder **what body did Christ have after Resurrection**? and why the **resurrection process take 3 days?** why not 1-day or 2-days?

FREE BOOKS TO OUR READERS

Free books to our readers

War in Heaven came to Earth. Satan Rebellion:

https://dl.bookfunnel.com/ea12ys3dmk

Your Life in Heaven:

https://dl.bookfunnel.com/vg451qpuzs

GLOSSARY

Glossary

Conscious Mind: The part of the mind that is aware of governing thoughts and actions.

Depression: A mood disorder that triggers prolonged sadness and apathy.

Ego: A person's sense of self-importance; the part of the mind that constructs identity and is in charge of reality testing.

Emotional Freedom Technique (EFT): Also called 'tapping,' this is a form of therapy for potent stress relief.

Energy Healing: A type of holistic therapy that uses the body's energy circuits to facilitate healing by unblocking energy tracks and identifying problems before they manifest as pain or illness.

External Manifestation: Events and occurrences that enter a person's reality from an outside source.

Higher Power: Refers to a divine, supreme being or other conception of God.

Internal Manifestation: Events and occurrences that enter a person's reality and stem from inside of them.

Karma: The sum of all actions in this and previous lifetimes that decide a person's destiny or fate in a future lifetime.

Mantra: A sound, word, or phrase that is repeated in meditation.

Meditation: A mind and body practice to increase calmness, relaxation, psychological balance, and overall well-being.

Metamorphosis: The transformation process that matures a being in distinct, unique stages.

Positive Disintegration: A theory of personality development where anxiety and tension are necessary for personal growth.

Post-Traumatic Stress Disorder (PTSD): A mental health disorder that stems from a traumatic event and is characterized by distress, anxiety, flashbacks, and intrusive thoughts.

Psychosomatic: Refers to symptoms that are caused by the interaction between the body and the mind, a physical response to a mental health issue.

Sound Healing: A form of therapy that uses music and frequencies to balance a person's energy in the body and mind.

Source: The non-physical, conscious energy of creation that can be attracted and aligned to.

Spiritual Awakening: The experience of collapsing your sense of separation from the oneness that usually begins with dissolving the ego.

Spiritual Evolution: The idea that the spirit evolves from a simple form that is ruled by nature to a higher form that is ruled by divinity.

Subconscious Mind: The part of the mind not presently in focused awareness.

Synchronicity: When events that have no causal connection occur simultaneously and appear significantly related.

Trauma: A deeply disturbing, stressful experience that may include physical injury or emotional shock and can lead to long-term neurosis.

Unconscious Mind: The deep recesses of a person's memories and past.

REFERENCES

References

7 omens that herald the Dark Night of the Soul. (2020, October 2). LonerWolf.

12 things not to do if you're suffering from depression. (n.d.). Intrepid Mental Health. –

18 signs you're experiencing a Dark Night of the Soul, otherwise known as an existential crisis. (2017, February 9). Thought Catalog.

A Dark Night of the Soul and the discovery of meaning. (n.d.). Kosmos Journal.

A flicker of faith. (2016, January 15). Ram Dass.

Abraham Lincoln Quotes. (n.d.). Quote Fancy.

Blaize, A. (2020, June 10). The Dark Night of the Soul. Law of Connections.

Boomer, S. (2020). What is your soul's journey (and where is your final destination?). Awake and Align.

156

Brown, M. (n.d.). [Silhouette of window vane]. Pexels.

Davis, L. (2016, July 9). *How your emotions are causing you physical pain, science explains.*

Depression or Dark Night of the Soul? (2021, September 28). Soul Shepherding.

Eckhart, M., & Stryz, J. (2003). The Wisdom of Meister Eckhart. New Grail.

Eckhart on the Dark Night of the Soul. (2018, April 2). Eckhart Tolle | Official Site - Spiritual Teachings and Tools for Personal Growth and Happiness.

Frontline. (n.d.). *The Long Walk of Nelson Mandela* [Video].

Gibran, K. (2012). Broken Wings. Bottom Of The Hill Publishing.

Googins, D. (n.d.). On the Other Side of Suffering is Greatness. YouTube.

Joyful confidence in God: the Dark Night of the Soul. (n.d.). Faith Gateway. http

Meyer, J. (2018). Battlefield of the Mind Study Guide: Winning the Battle in your Mind. Faith Words.

May, G. G. (n.d.). The Dark Night of the Soul. Spirituality & Practice.

Mcnutt III, S. (2018). Care Package : A Path to Deep Healing. Success Is A Choice.

Myss, C. M. (2004). Anatomy of the Spirit, and Why People Don't Heal and How They Can. Gramercy Books.

Nelson, B. (2019). The Emotion Code : How to Release Your Trapped Emotions for Abundant Health, Love, and Happiness. St. Martin's Essentials.

Nietzsche, F.W. & Common, T. (2021). Thus Spake Zarathustra. Binker North.

Norton, B. (n.d.). Why suffering is required for spiritual growth (Healing Depression, Anxiety, and Trauma [Video]. YouTube.

Onkka, L. (n.d.). Heal yourself and end suffering with [Video]. YouTube.

Press, J. (2022, February 26). The Dark Night of the Soul: understanding amidst the absence of meaning. Medium.

Project Life Mastery. (n.d.). How to free yourself from emotional pain & suffering [Video]. YouTube.

Richo, D. (1991). How to Be an Adult : A Handbook on Psychological and Spiritual Integration. Paulist Press.

Ritt, M. J., Hill, N., Cypert, S. A., & Sartwell, M. (2007). Napoleon Hill's Positive Action Plan: 365 Meditations for Making Each Day a Success. Plume.

Sadhguru. (n.d.). How do you eliminate suffering when suffering is all that you have left? [Video]. YouTube.

Salmansohn, K. (2001). How to Be Happy, Dammit : A Cynic's Guide to Spiritual Happiness. Celestial Arts.

TEDx Talks. (2015). Healing illness with the subconscious mind | Danna Pycher [Video]. YouTube.

Tolle, E. (n.d.). Simple Recipe for Overcoming Suffering [Video]. YouTube.

Understanding the dark night of the senses & the soul. (n.d.). The Young Catholic Woman.

What was Paul's thorn in the flesh? (2 Corinthians 12). (2021, December 29). Crossway.

Whyte, D. (2011). The House of Belonging: Poems. Many Rivers Press.

Wilde, O., & Holland, M. (2007). Oscar Wilde: A Life In Letters. Carroll & Graf.

Words, C. (2014, April 17). "Sweet Darkness" by David Whyte. Words for the Year.

Zebian, N. (2018). The Nectar of Pain. Andrews Mcmeel Publishing.

ABOUT AUTHOR

Trinity is a multi-award-winning author and a spiritual warrior. While life might not always work out according to plan, Trinity was able to take valuable lessons from each new experience. Trinity grew and developed and now shares a passion for enlightening others on spiritual knowledge in the hopes of closing the gap between Heaven and Earth. Trinity's writings reflect the depths of a passion and desire to connect with everyone seeking spiritual growth and education.

You can learn more at www.RocketshipPath2God.com or @ https://www.facebook.com/TrinityRoyalBooks